EVERY MAN'S DE
EVERY WOMAN'S

TONY EVANS
KINGDOM MAN

Lifeway Press®
Nashville, Tennessee

Published by Lifeway Press®
© 2012 Tony Evans • Transitioned to Video on Demand April 2022

ISBN 978-1-0877-7619-4 • Item 005840637

Dewey decimal classification: 305.31
Subject headings: MEN \ LEADERSHIP \ CHRISTIAN LIFE

Scripture quotations are taken from the Holman Christian Standard Bible®, Copyright © 1999, 2000, 2002, 2003, 2009 by Holman Bible Publishers. Used by permission. Holman Christian Standard Bible®, Holman CSB®, and HCSB® are federally registered trademarks of Holman Bible Publishers.

To order additional copies of this resource, write to Lifeway Resources Customer Service; 200 Powell Place, Suite 100; Brentwood, TN 37027; fax 615-251-5933; phone toll free 800-458-2772; order online at Lifeway.com; or email orderentry@lifeway.com.

Printed in the United States of America

Groups Ministry Publishing • Lifeway Resources
200 Powell Place, Suite 100 • Brentwood, TN 37027

Contents

About the Author

Dr. Tony Evans

DR. TONY EVANS is one of America's most respected leaders in evangelical circles. He's a pastor, a best-selling author, and a frequent speaker at Bible conferences and seminars throughout the nation. He has served as the senior pastor of Oak Cliff Bible Fellowship for more than forty years, witnessing its growth from ten people in 1976 to more than ten thousand congregants with more than one hundred ministries.

Dr. Evans also serves as the president of The Urban Alternative, a national ministry that seeks to restore hope and transform lives through the proclamation and application of God's Word. His daily radio broadcast, *The Alternative with Dr. Tony Evans,* can be heard on more than 1,300 radio outlets throughout the United States and in more than 130 countries.

Dr. Evans holds the honor of writing and publishing the first full-Bible commentary and study Bible by an African-American. A former chaplain for the Dallas Cowboys, he's currently the chaplain for the NBA's Dallas Mavericks, a team he has served for more than thirty years.

Through his local church and national ministry, Dr. Evans has set in motion a kingdom-agenda philosophy of ministry that teaches God's comprehensive rule over every area of life, as demonstrated through the individual, family, church, and society.

Dr. Evans is married to Lois, his wife and ministry partner of more than forty years. They are the proud parents of four—Chrystal, Priscilla, Anthony Jr., and Jonathan—and have a number of grandchildren.

Greatness
Is Your Destiny

There are plenty of males in the world today who are content to slide through life, never making any waves in the world around them. *Responsibility, leadership,* and *initiative* are foreign concepts to them. And the world is suffering for it.

Our world is falling apart, not from the lack of males but for the lack of men. Real men. Kingdom men. Men who recognize that God has uniquely endowed them with the capacity and destiny for greatness. A kingdom man understands and loves this. He doesn't run from responsibility; he runs toward it. This is the kind of man the world needs.

But the world isn't the only one crying out for kingdom men. God is too. He's looking for men who are willing to fully align themselves under His comprehensive rule. When they submit to His authority as their Lord, they are then willing to lead their families, businesses, and churches well. When a kingdom man shows up, everyone in his sphere of influence is affected for the better.

The time for the return of kingdom men has never been more critical. Our families need them. Our neighborhoods need them. Our churches need them. Our world needs them.

This study is the launching pad for that kind of man—the man you always suspected you might be. Over the next six weeks you will discover what a kingdom man is and the incredible responsibility God has given to him. You'll be challenged to live and do things you never before thought possible. And best of all, you'll learn the biggest advocate for your becoming this kind of man is God Himself.

If you're ready for the greatness God has destined you for, read on.
It's time for kingdom men to stand up and be counted.

Here's How It Works

This study includes both individual and group study. The best way to understand how to be a kingdom man is to engage in individual, daily devotions and to participate in a Bible-study group that includes video teaching and discussion.

Each week's study begins with a suggested process for a group experience. Each group session should follow this general outline.

- *"Get Started."* Each week will begin with a brief time of discussion that helps you and your group get to know one another better and discuss what the Lord has been teaching you during the previous week.

- *"Man Up."* Your group will watch a 30-minute video teaching segment while completing the viewer guide provided in each group experience. Next your group will follow the suggested questions to discuss the truths presented in the video. Then you will close with prayer.

- *"Hit the Streets."* Each week's group experience wraps up with a key verse of Scripture to memorize and specific challenges to tackle as you learn more about the tools God has given you for living as a kingdom man.

The teaching segment and discussion will provide a foundation for your individual study throughout the next week. Each day you'll read a devotion that fleshes out the Scriptures and ideas presented in your group. You'll also complete personal learning activities that will help you apply the principles of biblical manhood. The next week you'll come back to your group ready to begin another discussion based on the individual work you've done.

Throughout these six sessions you'll find yourself wanting things you never wanted, knowing things about yourself you never knew, and tackling obstacles you never imagined. I pray that these biblical truths about the man God has destined you to be will work their way deeply into your heart and that your family, workplace, church, and community will feel the influence of a man who's on fire for the kingdom of God.

Let's get to work.

WANTED:
KINGDOM MEN

In the game of basketball, the basket is set at 10 feet above the floor. For the game to be regulation, the rim is hung at this stationary height—the same height in any gym or on any playground around the world. But not every court is regulation.

You can purchase a basketball goal that sits in your driveway and has an adjustable height. This type of goal lets you raise and lower the basket according to your preference or your height so that even the shortest person can experience the thrill of slamming the ball through the hoop.

God has a standard. He has a goal. His kingdom is that goal. Yet many men have lowered His standard and then congratulated themselves for being able to dunk the ball. The results of this lowered standard affect many more people than just the men on the court. They affect us all. They show up in our country, our culture, and our world. It takes only a cursory glance around our homes, churches, communities, and globe to discover that men—maybe even most men—have missed the goal to live as kingdom men.

But God is on the hunt.
He's looking for a few good men.

WEEK ONE
Group Experience

Get Started

1. Introduce yourself and share one personal fact that will help your group get to know you better. Share what you hope to gain from this study.

2. Who have been the predominant male influences in your life?

3. What do you think is the most important characteristic of a kingdom man?

Man Up

Watch video teaching session 1 as you complete the viewer guide below.

To access the teaching sessions, use the instructions in the back of your Bible study book.

God's "third team" is a group of men whose job it is to ___represent___ Him and His kingdom on earth.

Kingdom men represent in time God's ___perspective___ from eternity.

The ___absent___ of kingdom men is bringing destruction, pain, and anguish throughout our land.

The cry for kingdom men is coming from the culture, from men themselves, and from ___Almighty God___. *Ez 22:30, Mal 4:6, Is 3:12*
___(Lord God)___

When God creates man, He is Yahweh Elohim: the powerful God who wants to ___relate___ to you and ___Oversees___ your affairs.

Gen 2:7-9, 15-16, 18

Gen 2:14-17

Addonai (Gives you the details.
Tell you what to do!

A kingdom man is a male who has learned to live his life under the _Lordship_ of Jesus Christ.

God's kingdom agenda is the visible manifestation of the comprehensive _rule_ of God over all of life. Ex 34:23-24

Malehood comes with birth.

Boyhood is when you are dependent, immature, and not yet responsible.

Manhood is when you are responsible enough to take care of someone else.

Chaos comes when God is not allowed to be God in the life of a man.

A woman is a _Mirror_ that lets a man know what his own submission to God looks like.

The goal of a kingdom man is to _implement_ the rule of God, not _create_ his own rules along the way.

A kingdom man understands that he is obligated to a _higher_ _order_. Ps 24:1

Discuss the video teaching with your group, using the questions below.

1. Where do you most clearly see the absence of kingdom men in the world today?

2. Why do you think so few men live their lives fully submitted to the lordship of Jesus Christ?

3. Tony described the stages of malehood, boyhood, and manhood. What stage do you honestly see yourself in?

4. If you are married, what does your wife's relationship with you reveal about your relationship with God?

5. What kinds of things would have to immediately change in your life if you became a kingdom man?

Close with prayer.

Hit the Streets

Scripture Memory

I searched for a man among them who would repair the wall and stand in the gap before Me on behalf of the land so that I might not destroy it, but I found no one. Ezekiel 22:30

➤ Pray by name every day this week for the men in your Bible-study group.

➤ In a journal write a description of the kingdom man you want to become. Include the way you want to function in your marriage, as a father, in your career, and in your church.

Read week 1 and complete the activities before the next group experience.

Day 1

Milk-Carton Men

I was walking through the various security checkpoints in a local prison where I was due to speak to a group of inmates. The scene was what I expected to see: guards, bars, weapons, and fences. But what struck me most on this particular day was the fact that each man confined behind these walls, at one point in his history, had been under the care of a man whose job it had been to lead.

Yet most of them had not only lacked a man to protect and guide them but had also suffered under the negative impact of men. In fact, roughly 70 percent of all prisoners come from fatherless homes. Approximately 80 percent of all rapists come from fatherless homes.[1]

Are these statistics surprising? Why or why not?

Outside the prisons the numbers are just as alarming. Fatherless homes produce 71 percent of all high-school dropouts and 63 percent of all teen suicides.[2] But a man doesn't have to physically leave to create a void in the home.

How might a father be physically present and yet still create a void in his home?

What might be some of the effects on the children?

In suburbia many fathers are missing in action through divorce, neglect, overindulging children in an effort to replace real parenting, putting their careers first, or loving the golf course more than their kids. Virtually every adult social pathology has been linked to either fatherless homes or homes with an absent, abusive, and neglectful man.

If those statistics fail to move you, let me see if I can punch you in the wallet. On average, taxpayers spend more than $8 billion annually on high-school dropouts for public-assistance programs like food stamps. High-school dropouts also earn an average of $260,000 less in their lifetimes than graduates, reducing our nation's earned taxable income by more than $300 billion annually. Teen pregnancies cost American taxpayers an average of $10 billion annually in public assistance, lost revenue, and health-care costs. Our prison population has increased 708 percent since 1972 to the highest per capita rate in the world. We now spend 1 of every 15 federal dollars on prisons. Are you starting to get it? Men—real kingdom men—are on the sides of milk cartons. They're missing, and we're all paying the price.[3]

Are you starting to get it? Men—real kingdom men—are on the sides of milk cartons. They're missing, and we're all paying the price.

Read Ezekiel 22:30.

I searched for a man among them who would repair the wall and stand in the gap before Me on behalf of the land so that I might not destroy it, but I found no one.

What was God looking for?

Kingdom men have been slowly disappearing for a long, long time. In the Book of Ezekiel we read that God released His judgment on a culture that was devoid of strong male leadership. Because no one would stand up and obey, He allowed the people of Judah to go their own way and choose their own idols. No man stood up before the people to lead them in the ways of God, and eventually God brought destruction to the nation.

If the almighty, omniscient God can't find a man to stand in the gap for an entire nation, then real men must be hard to come by. Oh, I'm sure there were plenty of males around. But kingdom men? Not so many of those. What about now?

If God made a thorough search for kingdom men around our nation and world today, would He still come up empty? In what ways would God want men to stand in the gap today?

Pray today that your heart will be open to conforming to God's definition of a kingdom man as you continue in this study. Express your desire to be the man He has made you to be.

Day 2

A Kingdom Man

Listen with me for a second. Can you hear the cry for a kingdom man?

It's in the heartbeat of every child who has been born or raised without a father. It's in every woman's dream that has been dashed by an irresponsible or neglectful man. It's coming from the homes, schools, neighborhood, states, and nations that have been shattered by the absence of kingdom men.

As a kingdom man, you have been commissioned by heaven to rule on earth. You represent the King. As His representative, there is much more to you than you may have even realized.

Read Jesus' words in Mark 1:15.

The time is fulfilled, and the kingdom of God has come near. Repent and believe in the good news!

Define *kingdom of God* in your own words.

The Greek word used for *kingdom* in the New Testament is *basileia,* which means *authority* and *rule.* The kingdom of God is the authoritative execution of His comprehensive rule in all creation. God's kingdom transcends time, space, politics, denominations, cultures, and all realms of society. The primary component on which any kingdom rests is the authority of the ruler. Without that there is anarchy. Chaos. A mess.

Read Genesis 2:15-25 in your Bible. Record the name of God that is used in these verses exactly as it appears in the text.

Now read Genesis 3:1. When Satan referred to God, what name did he use?

Genesis 2 contains several references to God, particularly in recording the way God related to Adam. For each one God is referred to as LORD God. Anytime you read the word *LORD* in all caps like that, it denotes the name God used for Himself: Yahweh. *Yahweh*, which literally means *Master and absolute Ruler*, is the name God used to reveal Himself to humankind.

But in Genesis 3 Satan used a different name for God. In verse 1 Satan asked Eve a seemingly innocuous question: "Did God really say, 'You can't eat from any tree in the garden'?" Notice that Satan didn't refer to God as the LORD God; instead, he stripped off the name LORD. Satan sought to remove God's titles of Master and absolute Ruler.

Why do you think Satan chose this particular way to refer to God?

How did that usage reveal Satan's plans and purposes?

It might not seem important at first glance, but Satan revealed his true character in the way he referred to God. By twisting God's name in a subtle but significant way, Satan sought to reduce God's rule over humankind. Satan kept the appearance of religion while eliminating divine authority. He's still doing the same thing today.

In what ways does the world deny God's absolute rule today?

How do believers and churches undermine God's rule?

Ever since Satan issued his challenge in the garden, there has been a continual battle over who will rule humanity.

Ever since Satan issued his challenge in the garden, there has been a continual battle over who will rule humanity. When men make decisions based on their own thoughts, beliefs, or values rather than on God's Word, they choose to rule themselves. They call the King God without recognizing His authority. Essentially, men become like Satan. Although they recognize the Creator's existence, they seek to dethrone Him.

Take a look at your life. Check any area in which you acknowledge God's existence without submitting to His authority.

☒ Family
☒ Social relationships
☒ Career
☒ Church or ministry
☒ Personal ethics
☒ Other:

☒ Community involvement
☒ Recreation and entertainment
☒ Hobbies

If we want to be kingdom men, we must fight hard against the tendency to dethrone our King. We've got to buck the trend of living under our own authority. A kingdom man is a male who places himself under the rule of God and lives His life in submission to the lordship of Jesus Christ. Instead of following his own way, a kingdom man seeks to know God's will and to carry out God's kingdom agenda on earth. When a kingdom man functions according to the principles and precepts of the kingdom, there will be order and provision. When he doesn't, he opens himself and those around him to chaos.

Pray through the definition of a kingdom man in the previous paragraph. Submit to your King any areas of your life you identified that are not under His authority.

Day 3

The First Man

It was all good. Everything. Without exception. In five days God created a spectacular earth with all of the features and amenities needed to live life to its fullest. On the sixth day God spoke forth His crowning achievement: man.

Read Genesis 1:26-28 and record God's actions.

"God _____" (v. 26).

"God _____" (v. 27).

"God _____" (v. 28).

God said it, God created it, and God blessed it. But specifically, God said, "Let Us make man in Our image, according to Our likeness. They will rule … " (v. 26). This verse communicates two key ideas. First there is the image of God.

What do you think it means to be made in the image of God?

How does being made in God's image influence the way you view your life and purpose on earth?

The plurality of "Let Us" and "Our image" refers to God's trinitarian nature. That is, God exists in three Persons from all eternity and to all eternity—Father, Son, and Holy Spirit. To be made in His image is to be a reflection of Him. Just as an automobile built in an assembly plant reflects the nature, purpose, and intention of its creator, humankind has been designed to reflect our Creator. That leads us to the second key element in this passage: man was created to rule.

Does God's command for man to rule mean that God no longer rules? How do God's rule and man's rule relate to each other?

When God created man in his image, He delegated to him the responsibility to care for and manage His creation. Up until that time God did all the work. He separated the water from the land, formed the light, grew the plants, created the sun and the moon, placed the stars in the sky, and made the animals. But on the sixth day, when God created man, He turned over the stewardship of the earth to the hands of men.

What is the difference between stewardship and ownership?

Why is that an important distinction?

Let's be clear. God has not turned over absolute ownership of the earth to men. But He has assigned to us the managerial responsibility for ruling it. God endowed men with the opportunity and responsibility to manage what He had made.

Read Genesis 2:15.

The LORD God took the man and placed him in the
garden of Eden to work it and watch over it.

Why did God place Adam in the garden?

**What implications does this verse have for the men God places
in particular situations today?**

Adam was placed in the garden to work it and watch over it. These two actions still hold true for the identity of men today. Despite the fact that you might moan every time the alarm clock goes off, going to work is not a bad thing. In fact, work is from God. It's part of your identity and responsibility as a man.

For Adam, working the land meant making it productive—developing its potential. From the productivity of the land, Adam would have what he needed to provide for those within his care. For men today, working the land means providing for those under our care. We also cultivate them, making sure they live up to all God has made them to be.

Adam was also to watch over the land. The Hebrew word used here means *guard* or *have charge of.* Every man is given a certain area—his garden—to care for and protect from threat. As with Adam, God's purpose is for each man to be responsible to cultivate and watch over what's within his care.

God's purpose is for each man to be responsible to
cultivate and watch over what's within his care.

What is your "garden"—the area you are responsible to care for and protect?

What are you doing to cultivate that garden?

What are you doing to watch over it?

Which of these functions do you sense that you need help with? Why?

Pray about the things and people God has put under your care. As you think about that responsibility, ask God for grace, courage, strength, and wisdom to cultivate and watch over what He has entrusted to you.

Day 4

Adam, Where You At?

It was a simple enough assignment: "Here's your garden. Work here to cultivate it. Take care of it and protect it." Pretty simple. But in Genesis 3 everything went haywire.

Read Genesis 3:1-7. Who was tempted in these verses?

Now read Genesis 3:8-9. Whom did the Lord look for in the garden?

If Eve initially ate the fruit, why did God look for Adam?

It's true that Eve ate the fruit. But curiously, when God came looking for the responsible party, it was Adam he called out to instead of his wife. Evidently, Adam was ultimately responsible. We read in the text, "The LORD God called out to the man and said to him, 'Where are you?'" (3:9). Notice that by using the name LORD God, the writer reasserted God's authority that Satan had tried to subvert. But also notice that God didn't call out, "Adam? Eve? Where are y'all?"

Even though Eve sinned first, the question was posed to Adam because he was the one responsible. Adam was accountable as God's assigned representative to carry out His agenda in the garden.

Instead of cultivating and protecting, Adam was the first man to exhibit a persistent problem that plagues the men of our day: silence. Up until this point Adam had been doing a lot of talking. He had been naming birds, cows, and fish. But when the snake showed up, Adam had nothing to say.

Now I know what you're thinking: *He wasn't there! What was he supposed to do, watch his wife day and night?*

You sure about that?

Read again Genesis 3:6. Where was Adam when Eve was facing temptation?

> *The woman saw that the tree was good for food and delightful*
> *to look at, and that it was desirable for obtaining wisdom.*
> *So she took some of its fruit and ate it; she also gave some*
> *to her husband, who was with her, and he ate it.*

Does that verse change your view of who was responsible for the first sin? How?

Despite the pictures you might have seen in a children's Bible, Eve wasn't alone and vulnerable. Her husband was standing right beside her. The whole time the snake was rapping, Adam was there—silent. Even when Eve turned to him and effectively deposed him as the leader of their home, Adam didn't say a thing. He just ate.

The disease of silence still afflicts men today. Who is speaking about the discipline of children in the home? Women. Who are the vocal leaders volunteering for leadership in the church? Women. Who is willing to take a stand against immorality in their families? Women. There are exceptions, but too many men operate just like Adam. When it's time to take a stand, they simply have nothing to say.

Do you feel tempted to remain silent when critical issues arise? Why or why not?

What does a man's silence say about his view of his role in the world?

First Adam was silent. Then he hid. In both cases Adam refused to embrace his God-given identity to rule well. Abdicating his authority, he became a follower instead of a leader. Then, when the responsibility finally caught up with him, he resorted to blaming his helpmate.

Read Adam's response to God's inquiry in Genesis 3:12.

*The woman You gave to be with me—she gave
me some fruit from the tree, and I ate.*

What are some ways men today try to shift blame to others?

The problem keeping many men in our culture today from being kingdom men is that they have relinquished their God-given right to rule, either through silence or blame. Instead of loving the fact that they are men and therefore are responsible by nature, they flee from their responsibility. And they always seem to find a reason not to own up to what it means to be a man. As a result, men have given up their opportunity to approach the Christian life as a challenge to conquer and rule well.

The problem keeping many men in our culture today from being kingdom men is that they have relinquished their God-given right to rule.

Ask God to show you any areas of your life in which you are not taking responsibility. Record them here.

Can I share the truth with you, friend? You're a man. As a man, you're responsible. You're to take the full responsibility to rule, under God's authority, for the blessing and benefit of everyone within the domain of your influence. You were created for this. It's time to reclaim your destiny.

Confess the areas you identified in which you have not taken responsibility. Ask God to forgive you and to give you boldness and wisdom to rule responsibly under His kingship.

Day 5

Reclaiming Manhood

The path to a better world starts with one kingdom man. I know what you're thinking: *The world is a big place.* That's true. But consider the potential influence of a single kingdom man. A kingdom man has the power to change his home, which changes his family. That family can initiate change in a church, which in turn can influence an entire community. That community can influence a state, which can then begin to impact the nation. All of this transformation can begin with one man who has fully aligned himself under the comprehensive rule of Jesus Christ.

Check the biggest obstacles to submitting your life to Christ's rule.

- ☒ Personal habits
- ☒ Family struggles
- ☒ Difficult relationships
- ☒ Lack of education
- ☐ Other:

- ☒ Limited influence
- ☒ Financial challenges
- ☒ Spiritual immaturity
- ☒ Misplaced priorities

Now think about the way God would respond to the obstacles you identified. Write one sentence that expresses what you think He might say.

Maybe you think your wife would never follow your leadership. Or your children would never respect your authority. Or you don't have enough influence in your community to make a real difference. I imagine the Israelites might also have had some objections when they heard what God had commanded them to do.

Read Exodus 34:23-24.

Three times a year all your males are to appear before the LORD God, the God of Israel. For I will drive out nations before you and enlarge your territory. No one will covet your land when you go up three times a year to appear before the LORD your God.

What practical objections might these men have raised when God told them that they had to leave their jobs, homes, and families three times a year?

Exodus 34 outlines the Israelites' covenant obligations to God. The chapter is full of commands about how to operate inside the land God would give to the people, and it describes the cyclical life Israel would lead. God instituted specific times each year, corresponding with the harvest, for the people of Israel to celebrate their heritage and to remember God's great works in their past.

When the people celebrated these festivals, they would not only remember the past but would also be encouraged about the future. These regular occurrences served as reminders of God's past, present, and future power and faithfulness.

If I were a farmer who lived off the land in a time when foreign powers threatened to invade and loot, I would probably be a little hesitant to leave my family and home to go to a meeting three times a year. I could easily justify skipping those times. I have to take care of things at home. I have to protect my family. I have to make sure everything keeps running properly. In fact, I might even argue that by requiring me to leave home, God was asking me to do something contrary to what it means to be a kingdom man.

How does Exodus 34:24 answer objections like these?

I will drive out nations before you and enlarge your territory. No one will covet your land when you go up three times a year to appear before the LORD your God.

Why would attending these meetings require faith on the part of the men of Israel?

God was saying to the men of Israel, "I got your back." Worried about your income? Don't worry. I got your back. Concerned about your family? I got your back. Thinking about the future? I got your back. When a man commits himself first and foremost to living under the rule of Jesus Christ, you can rest assured that God will take care of the rest.

When a man commits himself first and foremost to living under the rule of Jesus Christ, you can rest assured that God will take care of the rest.

If you're serious about being a kingdom man, all kinds of obstacles will stand in your way. Some of them might be practical. You might have to make difficult decisions about finances, time, and career. Others might be spiritual. You might have to make tough choices about your personal habits, your goals in life, and your approach to faith.

Being a kingdom man is hard that way. But God's got your back. Do you really think the Lord God is intimidated by any of these obstacles? If He can take care of invading armies, I'm pretty sure He can provide for you.

The only question is whether you're ready to take hold of your destiny and become the man you were created to be.

Present to God your biggest obstacles to becoming a kingdom man. Submit to His rule and profess your confidence in Him to bring the rest of your world in line with His lordship. Ask Him the first step He wants you to take in becoming a kingdom man.

1. Fathers Unite, "Fatherless Homes Now Proven Beyond Doubt Harmful to Children" [cited 1 December 2011]. Available from the Internet: *www.fathersunite.org/statistics_on_fatherlessnes.html.*
2. Ibid.
3. Bill Whitaker, "High-School Dropouts Costly for American Economy," 28 May 2010 [cited 1 December 2011]. Available from the Internet: *www.cbsnews.com/stories/2010/05/28/eveningnews/main6528227.shtml#ixzz1PNhtcbfg.*
4. C. Rouse, "Labor Market Consequences of an Inadequate Education" (paper presented at the symposium on the Social Costs of Inadequate Education, Teachers College, Columbia University, New York, NY, October 24, 2005).
5. Pew Center on the States, "One in 31: The Long Reach of American Corrections" (report for the Public Safety Performance Project, Washington, DC, March 2009).
6. The National Campaign to Prevent Teen and Unplanned Pregnancy, "Counting It Up: The Public Costs of Teen Childbearing" [cited 1 December 2011]. Available from the Internet: *www.thenationalcampaign.org/costs/.*
7. Pew Center, "One in 31."

GREATNESS
Is Your Destiny

Nothing can compare to the electricity, fully saturated with the smell of sweat, that permeates the air as towering men battle head to head and hand to hand in search of nothing but net. As the longest-tenured chaplain for any NBA team, having served the NBA champion Dallas Mavericks for more than three decades, I've become acutely familiar with the feel, smell, and taste of this atmosphere.

I love it. In fact, when I'm there, I grab it and hate to let it go. To say that passion dominates the mood would be an understatement. It's more like an urge—a pure ache for greatness.

While women fantasize about relationships, men fantasize about greatness. While women fantasize about cuddling, men fantasize about conquering. As men, we want to *be* something. We crave significance, influence, and impact. This desire for greatness shows up in the sports we play, the wilds we roam, and the movies we watch.

And can I tell you a secret? That's OK. In fact, greatness is your destiny.

Greatness is the reason you were created.

WEEK TWO
Group Experience

Get Started

1. Share one insight you gained as you completed week 1.

2. Were any of the statistics about the lack of a positive male influence particularly shocking or motivating to you? Which one(s)? Why?

3. Consider the tactics of Satan in Genesis 3. Have you ever been tempted to live as though God were not Lord? How?

4. Describe one kingdom man in your life. What makes him unique?

Man Up

Watch the video teaching for session 2 as you complete the viewer guide below.

To access the teaching sessions, use the instructions in the back of your Bible study book.

Ez 28:7
ISAIAH
Psalm 05

God created a lesser creature, man, in order to demonstrate His greater _____glory_____ .

Man was given the responsibility of _____ and _____ for his garden.

A kingdom man is a man who comes under the comprehensive ___rule___ of God.

The Devil kept "God" and dropped "___Lord___."

God created Adam and all the Adams since for ___greatness___ .

You were not created just to be a _____Male_____; you were created to be
a _____great_____ _____Man_____.

If you are a Christian, you have been chosen not only to be _____saved_____
in heaven but to be _____great_____ in history.

Whenever God used a man in the Bible, He always called them to do something
_____more_____ than they thought they could do.

God will make you _____Meek_____ so He can make you _____great_____.

The biggest Christian man is the one who has gone _____low_____ before God.

Greatness is when you achieve the _____reason_____ for which you were created
and maximize its _____influence_____ in the lives of others.

When you think about being a kingdom man, that
carries _____authority_____.

Discuss the video teaching with your group, using the questions below.

1. In what ways have you seen men in your life accept their responsibility
   for provision and protection?

2. In what ways have you seen men in your life fall short of that responsibility?

3. What is the difference between greatness in the kingdom of God and greatness
   in the world?

4. What specifically is holding you back from the destiny God has planned
   for you?

5. How might you daily remind yourself of your destiny as a man?

Close with prayer.

Hit the Streets

Scripture Memory

> *Whoever wants to become great among you must be your servant, and whoever wants to be first among you must be your slave. Matthew 20:26-27*

➤ Pursue greatness in your church this week by volunteering for a job no one else wants to do.

➤ Write a note of encouragement to your pastor, thanking him for his service.

Read week 2 and complete the activities before the next group experience.

Day 1

Why You Were Born

Stop what you're doing and go find a mirror. You there yet? Now tell me: what do you see? Maybe the hair isn't quite as thick as it used to be. Perhaps you're a little more round in the middle than you once were. Are you starting to show your age?

Now do me another favor. Look again, but this time look harder. Look deeper. Can you see it yet? There it is. Let me tell you what you're looking at.

Greatness.

Read Psalm 8. What three words would you use to characterize the mood of this psalm?

1.

2.

3.

What is it about man that made David praise God?

As a man, do you see yourself resembling the description in Psalm 8? Why or why not?

If you sense a little tension between these words and what you see in the mirror, you're not alone. It seems from Psalm 8 that David sensed it too. In verses 3-4 he turned his gaze upward, focusing on the vast expanse of the universe. Stars, planets, constellations—God made all of these as magnificent displays of His glory. For David, though, the greatness of creation only served to magnify the greatness God has given to every man.

> **Read Psalm 8:4-8 again in several translations. In what different ways is verse 5 translated?**

> **What do you think it means to be made a "little less than God" (v. 5)?**

Compared to the rest of creation, man is incredibly small. A speck. A spot. But the tininess of man serves to magnify God's greatness. David went on to say God chose this small speck of man to rule over His magnificent works. Man has all creation under his feet.

Who else but a great God could do something like this? Who else would be so powerful and glorious to trust little bitty men like us to steward the entire world? To put it another way, the glory and majesty God has given to man only serve to give greater glory and majesty to God. After all, just look at what God can do with something so small.

> **Why is it significant that glory and honor are given to every man?**

God has placed a crown on the head of man, thereby calling him majestic. You are majestic. You are royalty. You are awesome. It doesn't matter how athletic you are, how strong you are, what job you have, or how many people look up to you. Those things haven't earned your place in God's creation. He conferred that honor on you. He created you to be a kingdom man. It's in your DNA.

What is your response to the fact that God has given you the honor of being a kingdom man? Check any that apply.

☐ It's awesome to think God values me that much.

☐ I doubt that applies to me since I have no abilities God can use.

☐ I'm grateful God can use me to rule in His kingdom.

☐ I'm thankful being a kingdom man depends on God's grace and not on my abilities.

☐ Other:

When you become a kingdom man, you don't turn into something different; you simply embrace what God created you to be. You find the purpose for your creation.

The Enemy doesn't want you to know that. He doesn't want you to know God has given you glory, honor, and dominion to live out on earth. No, he'd much rather have you think you're nobody, you don't matter, and you have no say or influence. That way he can keep the kingdom of God from advancing, because those who've been given the legitimate authority to advance it have been lulled into thinking they lack significance and authority.

At some point you may have lost the leverage of your destiny and authority. Maybe through poor decisions or neglect, you've forgotten what it means to be a man. But it's never too late to wake up.

Use Psalm 8 as a guide as you pray today. Praise the name of the Lord for His creation and for creating you to rule in His kingdom. Ask Him to awaken you to your true identity as a kingdom man as you continue in this study.

Day 2

A Man's Dominion

When God created man in His image, He delegated to him the responsibility of caring for and managing His creation. In fact, God gave a mandate to man when He created him in His image: "They will rule" (Gen 1:26). Through this mandate God assigned man to manage what He had created.

Read Psalm 24:1.

The earth and everything in it,
the world and its inhabitants,
belong to the LORD.

How does God's rule of the earth, and everything it contains, relate to His directive for man to rule?

Though God hasn't turned over absolute ownership of the earth to man, He has willingly released some amount of direct control to us to manage the affairs of history. He has established a process, within certain boundaries, through which He allows man to make decisions. God respects those decisions even if they aren't in the best interests of His kingdom or of what's being managed.

You might think of it like this. The bank may own the house you live in, but you have the responsibility to pay a monthly mortgage on the house you say you own, as well as to maintain it. Though the bank doesn't get involved with the everyday duties of running your house, it doesn't give up the ultimate ownership of the house just because you live in it and manage it. But if you don't make your payments, you will lose your home.

In essence, God has delegated relative authority to man within the sphere of influence, or dominion, where He has placed each man.

How do you think most men feel about the privilege of ruling?

How do you know?

How often do you think about the dominion God has given you to manage and lead?

☐ Never   ☐ Sometimes   ☐ Daily

Describe a time when you felt the weight of your responsibility to rule.

Genesis 2 gives a picture of man's authority to rule. God gave Adam dominion and authority over every place he walked. He gave him the responsibility and privilege of caring for, cultivating, and protecting the garden. He even gave him the job of naming the animals. Consider the profound implications of that. Nothing, up to that point, had a name of its own. But once Adam named an animal, that was its name.

God respected the dominion He granted to Adam. But the dominion granted to man can have a negative effect as well as a positive one. Although God permits you a certain amount of authority, He expects you to rule in submission to His ultimate rule and in obedience to His commands. But He leaves you free to choose. Your decisions directly affect the quality of life within the sphere of your dominion. God didn't stop Adam from eating the fruit, and everything in his dominion was affected.

Your decisions directly affect the quality of life within the sphere of your dominion.

Read Genesis 3:16-19. List ways Adam's dominion was affected because of his choice to disobey God.

Now read Romans 8:19-22. What were some other effects on Adam's dominion because of his choice to sin?

Imagine how quickly Adam's domain changed. What had been joy was now frustration. What had been freedom was now drudgery. What had been peace was now chaos. Everything was affected: his wife, his daily chores, the animals. Adam had been given a great domain to manage. When he failed, his entire domain was turned upside down. The same is true when men fail to effectively rule their assigned domains today.

What effects do you see around you that have resulted from men's failure to lead?

As you look around the world today, you see a lot of men (maybe even most) bending under the weight of responsibility. Something inside tells us we were made to lead, to exercise authority and dominion. And yet when faced with that pressure, we're tempted to cut and run. You see it in the face of every child growing up in a home with an absent father and in the face of every single mother desperately trying to make it on her own.

> **Think about the sphere of influence God has given you.**
> **In what ways do you feel you're being faithful to carry out**
> **your responsibilities?**

> **In what ways do you feel you're failing to lead effectively?**

Although God is the sovereign and absolute King, He has given you an area to rule in His name, by His rules, and in His image as a kingdom man. You have been assigned a task, and it's a large task: to rule the sphere of influence where God has placed you in order to advance His kingdom agenda.

As a man, you have a charge to keep and a domain to rule. You have a specific realm in which God has positioned you to exercise dominion. The question is whether you're willing to take hold of it and use your God-given authority in the way He intended.

Consider in prayer the sphere of influence God has given to you. Pray for the people in your domain: your family, friends, coworkers, or employees. Surrender to God the areas in which you are failing to exercise your dominion. Tell Him you want to accept the responsibility He has given you to rule in His kingdom.

Day 3

Redefining Greatness

You were created for greatness, to rule an area of influence in which God has granted you management or dominion over. We need to address a couple of issues if we are to rule well as men. The first one comes in the form of a question: Isn't it prideful to think of yourself in terms of greatness? And doesn't God oppose the proud?

It's an important issue and a valid question. The simple truth is, that it doesn't sound very spiritual to say we look in the mirror and see a reflection of greatness. Can it really be that greatness is exactly what God wants for men in this world?

Read Matthew 20:20-28. What did the mother of James and John ask Jesus for in this passage?

Write in your own words the way Jesus responded to this request.

This was one proud, ambitious mother. She came to Jesus because she knew in her heart that her two boys were the greatest around. It was only right in her mind that they should be Jesus' number two and number three men. But Jesus needed to reeducate her about the way real authority and greatness are defined in the kingdom.

Interestingly, Jesus didn't give an answer that sounded very spiritual at first. Look back at Matthew 20. Did Jesus rebuke this woman for wanting her sons to be great? Did He rebuke James and John for wanting to be great? Look hard, because it's tough to see something that's not there. That's right. Nowhere in these verses do you see Jesus telling this mother and her boys that it was wrong for them to want greatness.

If the request for greatness wasn't wrong, what was wrong with this request?

Read God's promises to Abraham and David.

I will make you into a great nation,
I will bless you,
I will make your name great,
And you will be a blessing.
Genesis 12:2

I have been with you wherever you have gone, and I
have destroyed all your enemies before you. I will make
a name for you like that of the greatest in the land.
2 Samuel 7:9

Underline the common element in both of these promises.

God isn't opposed to greatness. In fact, the opposite is true: God is in favor of greatness. However, like James, John, and their mom, men today have a problem understanding what greatness truly is.

How do you think the world defines greatness?

Which one of the following choices are you most likely to associate with greatness?

- ☒ Power
- ☒ Wealth
- ☒ Position
- ☒ Educational degrees
- ☒ Possessions
- ☒ Talents and abilities

We commonly think of greatness in terms of power, wealth, and prestige. It's easy to recognize greatness because it's riding in the shiny new car or working on the top floor of the office building. Greatness has the fully funded 401(k) and owns the skybox at the arena. But in the kingdom of God, the definition of greatness is flipped upside down.

Read Matthew 5:3-12. How is the message of the Beatitudes similar to Jesus' teaching about greatness in Matthew 20?

In the Sermon on the Mount, Jesus took popular ideas about what it meant to be blessed and turned them on their heads: "You think you're blessed when you're rich? Wrong. Blessed are the poor. And you think you're blessed when you've got a full belly? Nope. Blessed are the hungry and thirsty. When everything's going right and everybody's your friend? That means you're blessed, right? Don't think so. You're blessed when you're persecuted."

Do you see it? In the kingdom of God there is a completely different value system at work. Similarly, greatness in the kingdom of God isn't defined like greatness in the world. True greatness isn't measured by how many employees you supervise or how big your bank account is.

Greatness in the kingdom of God isn't defined
like greatness in the world.

In Jesus' kingdom greatness is measured by service. God didn't give you a domain with people under your care so that you can be in charge and lord it over them. He assigned you this position so that you can serve the people in your realm of influence, leading them to connect with God and join His kingdom purposes. The greatest among us are the ones who are most willing to serve.

Ask God to show you specific ways you can serve those God has entrusted to you. Make a list of practical ways you can serve.

Day 4

Greatness Exercised

Greatness in the kingdom of God looks very different from greatness in the world. For a kingdom man, it's not about how high you can reach but how many people you can serve. That's at the core of Jesus' teaching in Matthew 20.

Read again Matthew 20:25-28. In what ways have you seen men dominate people?

Have you ever felt tempted to dominate others? If so, in what sphere of influence?

This leads us to the second issue we need to address in order to rule well. Anytime a man is given a great amount of responsibility for others, he may be tempted to exercise his authority for his own benefit rather than the benefit of those around him. When some men discover they're destined for greatness, given authority, and intended to rule, they see their identity as a license for others to serve them.

According to Jesus, nothing could be further from the truth. In the kingdom of God, where there's a radically different value system from the rest of the world, greatness is measured by service.

Are you starting to get the picture? A kingdom man exercises greatness in the kingdom from a position of service. When you take on some of the workload around the house, when you get up with a sick kid in the middle of the night, or when you volunteer for the least glamorous tasks at work or church, that's the pathway to greatness for a kingdom man.

> *A kingdom man exercises greatness*
> *in the kingdom from a position of service.*

In the world great men have people who do the menial tasks for them. But great are the toilet scrubbers in the kingdom of God! Jesus, never one to teach without modeling, showed us what true greatness looks like.

> **Read John 13:1-5,12-17. How do you think you would have responded if you had been in the room that night?**

> **How do Jesus' actions in John 13 relate to His teaching in Matthew 20?**

At a time in history when people walked almost everywhere on dusty, dirty roads, it would be difficult to imagine a more tangible display of servitude than to wash feet. Here we see the Son of God sinking to the depths as he scrubbed dirt and other nasty stuff off the feet of His followers.

Then comes the punch line: "A slave is not greater than his master, and a messenger is not greater than the one who sent him" (John 13:16). If Jesus, God the Son, is not too good to wash some feet, then neither are you. A kingdom man knows this.

But even more than that, a kingdom man *loves* this. He knows the way to be great is through a washbasin and a rag. It's in the dust and dirt of service. It's down there doing the things nobody wants to do but have to be done. The men who jump at the chance to follow Jesus' example are great in the kingdom.

In what ways are you currently serving others in the following areas?

Marriage:

Parenting:

Job:

Church:

Jesus didn't stop at washing feet. Though He was God, He

did not consider equality with God
as something to be used for His own advantage.
Instead He emptied Himself
by assuming the form of a slave,
taking on the likeness of men.

*And when He had come as a man
in His external form,
He humbled Himself by becoming obedient
to the point of death—
even to death on a cross.
Philippians 2:6-8*

So what about you? Are you too good to wash some feet? Is that beneath you? I hope not, because if it is, you might be a male, but you're very far from being a kingdom man. Be great today. Be great by bowing low.

What is one practical way you can serve in the following areas that you aren't currently doing?

Marriage:

Parenting:

Job:

Church:

Thank Jesus for leading the way in greatness through service. As you serve others in your domain of influence, remember that Jesus served sacrificially, even to the point of death.

Day 5

Accessing
Your Authority

God created you for greatness, and He intends that you manage well, under His authority, your particular sphere of influence. But maybe you're still looking around your family, your workplace, your church, and your community, and you're just not seeing it. You don't have the respect you think you need in order to rule. Or maybe *authority* seems like a foreign term in your life.

Don't be fooled by your eyes. Look beyond mere sight. When you do, you'll see that you don't need anything more from God than what He's already given you. Instead, you need to access what God has already authorized you to do.

Read Ephesians 1:3.

Praise the God and Father of our Lord Jesus Christ, who has blessed us in Christ with every spiritual blessing in the heavens.

What kinds of spiritual blessings has God already blessed every believer with?

Kingdom men today don't have an authority problem. We don't have a blessing problem. We have a perception problem. We already have every spiritual blessing through Christ Jesus: forgiveness, redemption, a position in His kingdom, an eternal inheritance, healing, spiritual power, and so much more. That's why Paul prayed "that the perception of your mind may be enlightened so you may know what is the hope of His calling, what are the glorious riches of His inheritance among the saints" (Eph. 1:18). Paul didn't pray that the Ephesians would get something else they lacked. Instead, he prayed that their eyes would be opened to what God had already given them.

Not only has God said you are to rule and lead in your domain, but He has also given you all you need to do it. It's a truth expressed well in 2 Corinthians 9:8: "God is able to make every grace overflow to you, so that in every way, always having everything you need, you may excel in every good work."

In Scripture God had a funny way of declaring things to be that didn't yet appear to be. When Abraham was old and childless, God told him that he would be the father of a great nation (see Gen. 12:1-2). When the Israelites were about to enter the promised land, God told them He had already given it to them (see Josh. 1:3-5). And when God sent Moses to confront Pharaoh, He had already granted Moses all the authority and power he needed to accomplish God's will.

Read Exodus 7:1-2.

The LORD answered Moses, "See, I have made you like God to Pharaoh, and Aaron your brother will be your prophet. You must say whatever I command you; then Aaron your brother must declare it to Pharaoh so that he will let the Israelites go from his land."

In what sense do you think Moses was to be like God to Pharaoh?

God gave Moses the enormous task of delivering the Israelites from bondage in Egypt. Leading the Israelites to freedom was in Moses' dominion. It was in the sphere of influence—the garden—where God had placed him. But God didn't just send Moses out. First He empowered Moses to accomplish His will and purpose.

At first Moses raised all kinds of objections about his assignment. "Who am I that I should go to Pharaoh and that I should bring the Israelites out of Egypt?" (Ex. 3:11). "What if they won't believe me and will not obey me but say, 'The LORD did not appear to you'?" (4:1). "Please, Lord, I have never been eloquent—either in the past or recently or since You have been speaking to Your servant—because I am slow and hesitant in speech" (4:10).

Moses thought he had an authority problem. Who am I to lead? Who am I to exercise authority? Who am I to carry out this plan?

> **What kinds of questions or doubts do you have about leading in the domain where God has placed you?**

You might have the same kinds of questions Moses did: *Who am I to lead my family? I've messed up so many times in the past. Who am I to exercise authority in the church? I don't have enough knowledge. Who am I to stand for God in the workplace? No one will listen to me.*

But just like Moses, we don't have an authority problem. We have a perception problem. God told Moses that He was going to make him "as God to Pharaoh" (Ex. 7:1) even though everyone thought Pharaoh was running the show. Yet God trumps everyone, and when God sends a man into the domain He's declared for him to rule, He empowers him to do just that. God didn't make Moses *be* God; He made Moses "as God to Pharaoh," meaning He gave him authority, even over someone who seemingly held earthly authority over Moses.

When God sends a man into the domain He's declared
for him to rule, He empowers him to do just that.

Because God had provided what Moses needed to accomplish the task, what was left for Moses to do?

This is the point where faith steps into the equation. But faith isn't measured by your mind nearly as much as it's measured by your feet. Moses was given the authority he needed, but he had to be willing to step back into Egypt to access that authority.

Men too have been given what they need to lead well in their domain. If you truly believe God has granted you all you need, it's time to take a step. You must begin to speak, walk, and live with authority. When you're willing to do that, you demonstrate that you truly believe what God says.

Faith is taking responsibility. It means exercising the authority God has already given you. Today's the day. Start leading.

Pray, using Ephesians 1:3 as a guide. Thank God for the resources He has already given you in His Son, Jesus Christ. Pray for the faith and courage to start living out that belief.

Claiming Your TERRITORY

The church I pastor has a motion-detector lighting system, which automatically turns off the lights in a room if no one is present for a certain number of minutes. When someone walks into the vicinity of the motion detector, the lights come back on.

In many ways the motion-detector lighting system pictures a kingdom man's practice of his right to rule. The electric company has supplied all of the electricity needed to fully power every light in our buildings, but that power doesn't come on until motion is detected. No motion, no lights.

Similarly, God has provided each man everything he needs to exercise his authority. But just as with the motion-detector system, motion is required to witness the power that's available.

For a kingdom man, the question isn't one of power or authority. It's one of motion.

It's time to start claiming the territory
God has granted you.

WEEK THREE
Group Experience

Get Started

1. Share one insight you gained as you completed week 2.

2. Why does the Enemy want you to forget that God has created you with glory, honor, and dominion?

3. Describe the dominion God has entrusted you to lead. How, as a kingdom man, are you meant to exercise authority over it?

4. What is a kingdom man's family supposed to feel when he is rightly exercising his authority?

Man Up

Watch the video teaching for session 3 as you complete the viewer guide below.

To access the teaching sessions, use the instructions in the back of your Bible study book.

God has decided to do most of what He does based on the _____ we make.

God now must stand with you and for you and in support of you because you are _____ with Him.

Every man has a divine _____.

God will only deliver that destiny when you're ready to _____ it.

There's no man who has reached his destiny without going through the _____.

Everything you need for where God is taking you, you _____ have.

God will _____ it, but you have to _____ it.

When you're a kingdom man, there is an _____ to claim because there's a _____ to fulfill.

Four Principles to Taking Your Destiny

1. Leave _____ behind.

Yesterday will _____ you, whether it's good, bad, or ugly.

2. Seize your _____.

God is waiting on us to _____ our movements toward Him under His rule so He can take us to what He has set up for us.

God responds to _____.

God is looking for movement. That movement is called _____.

3. Focus on _____, not people.

4. Stay tied to God's _____.

Kingdom men first ask, "What does _____ say about this matter?"

Discuss the video teaching with your group, using the questions below.

1. What kind of yesterday do you need to leave behind—good, bad, or ugly?

2. Why do you think God responds to motion rather than just words?

3. Do you struggle with focusing on God and not people? Which people in particular draw your focus away from God?

4. What practices do you need to introduce into your life to stay tied to God's Word?

5. What is one specific way the other men in your group can pray for you this week?

Close with prayer.

Hit the Streets

Scripture Memory

Praise the God and Father of our Lord Jesus Christ,
who has blessed us in Christ with every spiritual
blessing in the heavens. Ephesians 1:3

➤ Consider what experiences in your past are holding you back—good, bad, or ugly. Write them on a piece of paper; then bury them as a symbol of leaving them behind.

➤ To stay tied to God's Word, find a daily-Bible-reading plan online or at a Christian bookstore. Make room for a daily devotion in your schedule.

Read week 3 and complete the activities before the next group experience.

Day 1

Take the Land

The Book of Psalms reveals the fullness of the rule entrusted to humankind:

The heavens are the LORD's,
but the earth He has given to the human race.
Psalm 115:16

We were created to manage this third rock from the sun, for good or for bad. It has been given to the sons of men. But just because something is given doesn't mean it is taken. Even though God has provided you with everything you need to maximize your life and everyone else's within your sphere of influence, He won't make you do it. He will equip you, but He won't force you. Every man must take responsibility and initiative.

At the same time, God's Word clearly tells us:

Wait for the LORD;
be strong and courageous.
Wait for the LORD.
Psalm 27:14

Waiting for the Lord doesn't mean to sit down and do nothing. If you're waiting on the Lord for a job, you don't sit at home all day looking at the phone. If that's all you do, you'll be waiting for a very long time. That's passive waiting.

God wants active waiting. You ask the Lord for a job, and you believe, in His time, He will provide that job. Because you believe, you get up, get dressed, and go out and look for what you believe God has provided for you. By being active in your waiting, you exercise faith. You believe so strongly that God's going to do what He said He would do that you actively look to find just how His provision is going to come.

Read Jesus' words in Matthew 6:26.

*Look at the birds of the sky: They don't sow or reap
or gather into barns, yet your heavenly Father
feeds them. Aren't you worth more than they?*

How do birds demonstrate how to actively wait on God?

A bird doesn't create or provide its own food, but it still has to do something to get the food that's been provided for it. A bird can't just sit on a branch with its beak wide open, waiting for God to drop in a worm from heaven. Instead, the bird needs to look for a worm, a bug, or a seed that God has provided.

Describe in your own words the difference between active and passive waiting.

What are you waiting on from God?

Is your waiting active or passive?

It's one thing to acknowledge intellectually that effectively leading your home, church, and community is God's will. It's another thing to believe it so strongly that you actually begin to walk in God's will as a kingdom man.

If you're just waiting for your wife, kids, church, or friends to align themselves under the rule of Christ, you're going to be waiting a long time. You'll be like a starving bird sitting on a limb, looking up to heaven, and wondering when the worms are going to drop. This kind of faith is no faith at all. James 2:17 says, "Faith, if it doesn't have works, is dead by itself." If you believe God's destiny for you is to be a kingdom man, start acting like a kingdom man.

You can do that by starting to take what God has already given you. A kingdom man moves according to what God's instructed him to do, thus ruling his world rather than allowing everything and everyone else to rule him. Be a man of movement.

A kingdom man moves according to what God's instructed him to do, thus ruling his world rather than allowing everything and everyone else to rule him.

Read Joshua 1:1-9. What phrase did God repeat to Joshua over and over?

Why do you think God chose to emphasize that phrase?

What types of emotions might Joshua have felt?

Joshua 1 records a pivotal time in the history of Israel. In this passage the nation, after 40 years of wandering in the desert, had finally come to the border of the land God had promised to Abraham centuries before. They were on the edge of their destiny, poised to cross over the Jordan River.

Imagine the sense of excitement around the camp. The land their parents and grandparents and great-grandparents had longed for was within sight. The tents must have teemed with excitement about what was before them. But perhaps not everyone was excited.

Moses had led the people out of Egypt and through four decades of desert life. But now he was dead, and an untested leader named Joshua was taking over. His first assignment was to lead the people to their destiny, to claim what God had promised them. I'm sure Joshua was nervous, especially since the impenetrable fortress city of Jericho waited on the other side of the river.

Maybe that's why God reminded Joshua again and again to be strong and courageous.

What task might God be reminding you to be strong and courageous for today?

What are the immediate challenges waiting for you if you decide to be a kingdom man?

If you have the same feeling as Joshua—that the task is too big for you and the responsibility is too great—then you might find Joshua 1:3 particularly comforting. God told Joshua, "I have given you every place where the sole of your foot treads, just as I promised Moses."

That's right. The outcome isn't in doubt. God has already given you the land. He's already prepared the way for you to be a kingdom man. This is what He wants for your life. Your job is to be strong and courageous and cross the river.

Thank God for having already secured the victory for the battles you will face as a kingdom man. Pray for strength and courage to take possession of the land He has promised you.

Day 2

Leave Your Past Behind

If you want to claim your territory and take hold of your destiny, the first thing you must do is to leave the past behind. The past is like a rearview mirror. It's an important piece of equipment to have on your vehicle, but its purpose is to glance at and not to stare into. If you spend all your time looking at the rearview mirror, you'll never get where you need to go in one piece.

This was the first lesson for Joshua to learn before moving into the promised land.

Read Joshua 1:1-2.

After the death of Moses the LORD's servant, the LORD spoke to Joshua son of Nun, who had served Moses: "Moses My servant is dead. Now you and all the people prepare to cross over the Jordan to the land I am giving the Israelites."

What past did Joshua have to leave behind?

Why might it have been difficult for Joshua to do so?

Talk about some big shoes to fill. Joshua was taking the reins of leadership from Moses. Yep, *the* Moses—the man who brought down the plagues on the Egyptians, parted the Red Sea, and talked to God face-to-face. As if that weren't enough, consider the fact that Moses was the only leader anyone in the Israelite camp had ever known. Their parents had followed Moses out of slavery, and every day since then for the past 40 years the people had looked to him for guidance and direction.

Understandably, Joshua might have been intimidated by this huge task. Joshua could have spent the rest of his life questioning his every move, always looking over his shoulder, focusing on the past. That's why, right out of the gate, God reminded Him, "Moses My servant is dead" (v. 2).

Translation? "Leave the past behind, Joshua. Move forward." Joshua needed to be reminded that although Moses had been a great man and a great leader, he had not gotten them into the promised land. Moses was yesterday, and it was time for Joshua to get up and move on.

Maybe you haven't reached your destination yet because you're still tied to Moses. In order to move forward and realize what God has in store for tomorrow, it's important that you say good-bye to yesterday, whether it was good or bad.

> **Is it difficult for you to leave your past behind? If so, check any reasons that apply.**
>
> ☐ **The past holds successes I want to cherish.**
>
> ☐ **I can't seem to let go of my past failures; they keep me from moving forward.**
>
> ☐ **I feel more comfortable dwelling on past achievements.**
>
> ☐ **I'm hesitant to move forward because I'm afraid of failing.**
>
> ☐ **I'm holding back because I don't want to accept more responsibility.**
>
> ☐ **Other:**

Perhaps it's difficult for you to leave the past behind because you've left a trail of chaos where you've been. Maybe you've been living in boyhood instead of graduating to manhood. Or maybe you've shirked responsibility and authority, and your family and friends have suffered because of it. Maybe you're still feeling the practical effects of your past, such as paying child support from a broken marriage or watching your kids drift further and further from you.

All of these reasons make it both emotionally and practically difficult to let go and move forward. But hear these words from the Lord, just as Joshua heard them: "Moses is dead." You can't change the past. But you can move into the future.

You can't change the past. But you can move into the future.

What's a negative decision or experience that you need to move beyond?

What's keeping you tied to that experience?

How can you actively try to let it go?

On the other hand, maybe you've been a virtual superman up to this point. Looking back brings you great satisfaction because you've been living a life fully aligned under the lordship of Jesus. However, yesterday's victories will not carry you through today. Past successes can keep you frozen in the past just as effectively as failures can. With successes you might be tempted to think the hard work is done and slip into a state of pride over what you've done or laziness about the tasks that remain. You've got to let go of yesterday's successes too.

What past successes are you clinging to?

What danger might there be in dwelling on your past successes?

Paul put this in perspective for us in Philippians 3:13-14: "Brothers, I do not consider myself to have taken hold of it. But one thing I do: Forgetting what is behind and reaching forward to what is ahead, I pursue as my goal the prize promised by God's heavenly call in Christ Jesus." Paul knew about letting go of both successes and failures. Before he met Jesus on the Damascus road, Paul had plenty of failures. An ardent enemy of the church, he had persecuted and killed Christians. A person can't fall much lower than that.

But after becoming a Christian, Paul had traveled the known world sharing the gospel. He had put his academic prowess to good use, arguing extensively for the faith and writing the bulk of what we know today as the New Testament. Remarkably, neither his great failures nor his tremendous successes bogged Paul down. He knew that each could be like a weight tied to his feet. That's why he made it his practice to forget what was behind.

Here's something else I love about Philippians 3:13-14: the reason Paul forgot what was behind was that he was so incredibly focused on what was ahead. The goal for which Christ called him dwarfed anything in his past. Like a runner straining out in the last few yards of a race to burst through the finish line, Paul focused forward on what God had for him next.

> Has God revealed a future goal for you in the domain where He has appointed you to rule? If so, describe the direction in which He is leading you.

God is calling you forward. He's calling you to take hold of your inheritance, authority, and domain. But you'll never get there if the past is weighing you down. It's time for you to have a funeral for yesterday.

Talk to God about your past failures and successes. Be specific about the things you need to leave behind. Ask Him to give you such a tremendous vision for tomorrow that your yesterday begins to fade in comparison.

Day 3

Seize Your Spiritual Inheritance

God told Joshua to forget the past. Moses was dead. Have a funeral for yesterday. But that's not all He told him. If you want to claim the territory given to you and start living your destiny, God said, you must also seize your spiritual inheritance.

Read God's further instructions to Joshua.

Now you and all the people prepare to cross over the Jordan to the land I am giving the Israelites. I have given you every place where the sole of your foot treads, just as I promised Moses. Your territory will be from the wilderness and Lebanon to the great Euphrates River— all the land of the Hittites—and west to the Mediterranean Sea.
Joshua 1:2-4

What in this passage do you think would have inspired confidence in Joshua?

God told Joshua that He had already marked out where he was supposed to go. He had already staked out his inheritance. He told Joshua He had set aside the land from the wilderness to "the great Euphrates River" and "west to the Mediterranean Sea."

Notice that God didn't say He was going to give the Hebrews this land. He said He had already given it. By using the past tense, God emphasized this was their land. It was their domain. God had already given them the land and the people in it even before Joshua had set foot there.

What was true for Joshua and the Israelites is also true for you today. God has already given you everything you are destined to have. But also like Joshua, you have a part to play in actualizing what God has given you.

Look back at Joshua 1:2-4. Even though God had already given him the land, what did Joshua have to do?

What must a kingdom man do, even though God has already given him everything he is destined to have?

To live a life of kingdom authority, Joshua actually had to go and get what God had already given. He had to move. If Joshua had stayed in the wilderness and never crossed the Jordan River, both he and the Israelites would've never gotten what God had granted them.

God has an inheritance and a destiny for you as well. But one reason you may not have experienced it yet is that your feet have not marched in tune with faith. God said to Joshua, "I have given you every place where the sole of your foot touches" (v. 3). In other words, God had given it, but Joshua had to go get it. He had to actually walk.

The Hebrew word used for "where the sole of your foot touches" is *darak,* and it refers to a press. It's the same word used to describe a winepress where grapes are trod on. Long before sophisticated machinery was created to turn grapes into wine, individuals collected grapes from the vineyard and then trod on top of them. They literally walked on the grapes to squeeze out the juice so that it could then be fermented and turned into wine. Treading on the grapes released what had been locked inside.

When a kingdom man starts walking in God's destiny for him, he isn't trying to get God to give him something. He's simply walking on what God has already provided for him in order to draw it out. This is what real faith is all about. Faith means you believe God so much that you act on what He says.

Faith means you believe God so much

that you act on what He says.

One reason more men aren't realizing what God has in store for them is either because they don't know He has something in store for them or they aren't taking the initiative to reach out and grab it. This is the normal process of receiving God's provision. It's true that sometimes God simply drops things into your lap without your doing anything. But most of the time, He works through the very ordinary act of obeying Him in whatever He has said to do. Then you see Him release the blessing He has planned for you.

Do you want to lead in your marriage? Then in faith start sacrificially loving your wife as Christ loves the church. Do you want your children to respect, obey, and follow you? Then in faith begin speaking kind words of direction, encouragement, and discipline to them. Do you want to see your influence grow in your community? Then in faith take the initiative to begin something that will benefit your community.

Paul wrote to Timothy, "Fight the good fight for the faith; take hold of eternal life that you were called to and have made a good confession about in the presence of many witnesses" (1 Tim. 6:12). The Greek word *epilambanomai*, translated "take hold," literally means *to seize*. Paul was telling Timothy to seize all that was contained in his salvation. Far too often it seems that men view the Christian life as a passive one in which they must live. Instead, we must view it as a gateway of opportunity to conquer life's challenges.

So get up. Stop whining. Stop blaming. Stop fearing. Get up and take some initiative. Start walking and go get what God has for you. The kingdom of God needs each man to get up and advance that kingdom together.

Identify any areas of your life where you have not seized what God has provided.

- ☒ **Marriage**
- ☒ **Parenting**
- ☒ **Career**
- ☒ **Community**
- ☐ **Other:**

- ☒ **Church**
- ☒ **Witnessing**
- ☒ **Ministry**

Check anything that has kept you from taking hold of what God has given you.

☒ Fear   ☒ Lack of knowledge
☒ Bad habits   ☒ Lack of confidence
☒ Lack of discipline   ☒ Comfort
☒ Lack of faith   ☒ Different priorities
☐ Insecurity about gifts and talents
☐ Uncertainty about what God wants me to do
☐ Other:

Pray about the obstacles keeping you from stepping out in faith where God has already provided for you. Pray for wisdom, strength, and courage to start treading on the land God has given you.

Day 4

Focus on God, Not People

God knew once Joshua put the past behind him and entered the promised land, he would face a large number of enemies whose goal would be to stop him from reaching his destination.

Read Joshua 1:5.

No one will be able to stand against you as long as you live. I will be with you, just as I was with Moses. I will not leave you or forsake you.

How do you think this promise changed the way Joshua approached these battles?

Yesterday we saw that God first told Joshua to get up. Now He told him to man up. The people in the land wouldn't like the fact that the Hebrews were moving in. Knowing Joshua would encounter tough opposition, God told him ahead of time that none of this resistance would be successful in preventing him from receiving what God had promised.

Unfortunately, many of us have let other people keep us from pursuing the fullness of God's purpose in our lives. Maybe they were bad, mean, or evil. Maybe they had more money, more power, or more influence than you. Maybe you stalled from moving forward because their comments and criticism made your life miserable.

If someone has threatened or blocked your access to the land God has given you, keep in mind that people, on their best day, are just people. And God, on His worst day, is still God. We can easily blow things out of proportion and conclude that people are more than people. But one of the greatest experiences you can have is watching God override people, especially those you thought were indomitable.

God told Joshua that no matter how much the Canaanites towered over them or how deeply the Hittites growled, no one would be able to stand before him and block him from getting where God said he was to go. You get into trouble when you start focusing on people rather than God. If you focus on people, you'll be intimidated and easily dissuaded. If you focus on God, you'll experience supernatural confidence and peace as you move out to claim your land of promise.

Just as Joshua encountered opposition, we shouldn't be surprised if we face opposition too. In fact, almost anytime God called someone in the Bible to move into His destiny for them, they faced opposition.

Identify some biblical characters who were obedient to God but met human opposition.

Is the opposition surprising to you? Why or why not?

Why do you think the people of God face opposition while obediently following Him?

It's inevitable that you'll face opposition, just as Noah, Abraham, Moses, David, Elijah, Peter, Paul, and even Jesus did before you. But why does it happen? More specifically, why does God allow it to happen?

Think about Joshua and the Israelites again. God had a place of destiny prepared and ready for them to occupy, and yet He didn't just zap the group of people living there into oblivion. If God just wanted to get His people into the land flowing with milk and honey, why didn't He remove the people who were already there? The rest of the Book of Joshua shows that God didn't do that. Instead, the people engaged in battle after battle to establish their nation.

The only conclusion we can draw is that God wasn't interested merely in getting His people into the promised land. He had another motive in mind.

Why do you think God wanted the Israelites to fight battles in conquering the promised land?

If given the choice, I'm sure the Israelites would have preferred the land to be vacant when they marched in. Likewise, none of us enjoy meeting opposition today. But there's an incredible amount of value in that opposition—at least from God's perspective. Sometimes opposition is the best classroom.

When something stands in your path—something far too big for you to handle—that's when you learn how to depend on God. That's when you learn about the nature of humility. That's when you learn about true provision. If you never met opposition, you'd never experience this kind of growth.

> *When something stands in your path—something far too big for you to handle—that's when you learn how to depend on God.*

If you are presently facing opposition in your effort to become a kingdom man, what are you learning about dependency on God?

What are you learning about humility?

What are you learning about God's provision?

God can bring about His good purposes for your life through opposition. God sees it as another opportunity to form you into the man He wants you to be. So you've got two choices: you can focus on people—the opposition—or you can focus on God. He has promised, "No one will be able to stand against you as long as you live. I will be with you. … I will not leave you or forsake you" (Josh. 1:5). When you focus on God, He will not only deliver you, but He will also form you more and more into a kingdom man through that deliverance.

Pray about the opposition you are facing in life. Pray for God's provision, power, and goodness to be evident in the way you respond to opposition. Ask God to help you stay focused on Him and to form you into the man He wants you to be through your experience.

Day 5

Stay Connected to God's Word

Joshua's predecessor, Moses, was never considered a military man. He was a prophet and a leader. But Joshua? He was different.

> **Read some of Joshua's background in Numbers 14:6-9. Based on this passage, how would you describe Joshua?**

The Israelites sent 12 spies into the land of Canaan. They came back telling stories of a wonderful land flowing with milk and honey. That was their way of saying the land was bountiful. It would no doubt be a place where the people could prosper.

But as good as the land was, the spies also reported fierce natives with impenetrable cities. Ten of those spies recommended that the Israelites turn back the way they had come. But two of the spies had a very different viewpoint. Sure, the men were big, but they weren't nearly as big as God. Joshua, a fighter, wanted to charge into the promised land and get the battle started.

Fast-forward 40 years. Now it was time for Joshua to lead the people into the land. As a strategist, he knew how to approach the enemy, invade the territory, and take the land. Yet God had a different word for him.

> **Read Joshua 1:6-9. Why do you think God gave this instruction about His Word to Joshua above all else?**

Before the battle began, God reminded Joshua to stay tied to His Word. He reminded him that his strength was found in God's presence with him, not in Joshua's war strategies. As a military man, Joshua would've been tempted to come up with his own methods for taking the land. But God reminded him that the way to experience success in the new land was to stay securely tied to the presence and Word of God.

> In what situations are you tempted to formulate your own tactics and invent your own solutions instead of relying on God's Word? Consider the examples below. If one applies to you, write the reason you tend to trust your skills and abilities in that situation.
>
> Financial decisions:
>
> Parenting:
>
> Career moves:
>
> Other:

God is unpredictable. He often accomplishes what He has purposed to do in a manner unlike what you or I or Joshua would have strategized. After all, he sent a brilliant military commander on a fool's errand of walking around a fortified city seven times, only to bring down the walls all by Himself.

If you're a kingdom man, your job isn't to make decisions on your own. It's simply to seek the will and ways of your King. It's not rocket science. Success in being a kingdom man comes when you master the skill of following God well.

> *If you're a kingdom man, your job isn't to make decisions on your own. It's simply to seek the will and ways of your King.*

In Scripture you'll find guiding principles for living and leading in your sphere of influence. When you start doing that, you'll also begin to see God working and moving in ways you never thought possible.

> Identify a past decision you made in which you wish you had consulted God's Word in advance. What difference would God's Word have made?

Now identify a time when God's Word guided you to a decision that reflected God's will for your life.

Notice that God reminded Joshua to "recite it day and night so that you may carefully observe everything written in it" (Josh. 1:8). The language here describes a continual tie to God's Word. You don't just read it, meditate on it, and put it into practice every now and then. You do so all the time. Reliance on the Word of God is your source of life.

Joshua needed to stay connected to God's Word to receive God's next instructions. God never again told him to attack a city the same way he attacked Jericho. Walking around the walls was one strategy for one particular moment. Thankfully, Joshua didn't say, "Well, it worked last time, so let's use it to conquer all of the cities." Instead, he understood that he needed to keep his eyes on God to know what his next steps should be. In the same way, we must stay tied to God's Word.

Check the statement that describes the current role of God's Word in your life.
☐ I read it every day and depend on it as my source of life.
☐ I read it every chance I get.
☐ I use it to get guidance when problems arise.
☐ I read it during my small-group Bible study.
☐ Other:

Kingdom man, let go of the past; seize your spiritual inheritance; focus on God instead of people; and stay tethered to His Word, even if that means marching around a city for seven days. When you do, you'll be ready to move into the destiny God has marked out for you.

Pray about your response to the previous activity. If you are not constantly reading God's Word and relying on it, ask God to give you a renewed love for His Word. Will you commit to read His Word each day and follow His instruction?

The Life of a
KINGDOM
MAN

If you're a messed-up man, you're going to contribute to a messed-up family. If you're a messed-up family, you're going to contribute to a messed-up church. If you're a messed-up church, you're going to contribute to a messed-up community. If you're a messed-up community, you're going to contribute to a messed-up state. If you're a messed-up state, you're going to contribute to a messed up-country. And if you're a messed-up country, you're going to contribute to a messed-up world.

The only way to have a better world made up of better countries composed of better states filled with better communities influenced by better churches and inhabited by better families is by becoming a better man. It starts with you.

The path to a better world begins with you.

WEEK FOUR
Group Experience

Get Started

1. Share one insight you gained as you completed week 3.

2. What is the difference between God's authority and your authority?

3. Why is waiting for God an active rather than a passive process?

4. What is the biggest lesson you learned from the account of Joshua's commission to seize the promised land?

Man Up

Watch the video teaching for session 4 as you complete the viewer guide below.

To access the teaching sessions, use the instructions in the back of your Bible study book.

One challenge for men today is _____.

Every Christian man is to do to Jesus what Jesus did to God: _____ himself.

Jesus was in perfect alignment with the _____.

A blessing is experiencing, enjoying, and extending the _____ of God in your life.

Whatever you want God to do _____ you, tell Him how you will use it _____ you.

_____ God is the foundational principle of God _____ in your life.

The fear of God opens up God's _____.

To fear God means to take God _____. To take God seriously means to relate to Him on His _____ rather than making Him come down to ours.

When we decide to take God seriously, we begin to see Him unfold His _____ and His _____ that He has destined for us.

God wants the total _____ of the man so that through the man and in the man He can express His will.

The world is an organized system, headed by _____, that leaves _____ out.

You are fearing God when you _____ in His _____.

If you begin to _____ in the fear of God and not merely _____ in the fear of God, then you have opened up the treasure chest to the _____ God has for you.

The Blessings of Fearing God

1. Your _____

2. Your _____

3. Your _____

If you are out of alignment, that which is _____ you will be out of alignment too. If you put God first, you will discover Him _____ on your behalf and _____ you in ways you never imagined.

Discuss the video teaching with your group, using the questions below.

1. Describe the concept of alignment in the life of a kingdom man.

2. What specific area of your life needs to be more aligned with God's rule?

3. What is God's ultimate purpose in blessing you? How can you remind yourself of the responsibility to extend the blessing to others?

4. What does it mean to fear the Lord? In what ways is your life failing to reflect your fear of God?

5. Which of the blessings of fearing God are most meaningful to you now? Why?

Close with prayer.

Hit the Streets

Scripture Memory

How happy is everyone who fears the Lord,
who walks in His ways!
You will surely eat
what your hands have worked for.
You will be happy,
and it will go well for you. Psalm 128:1-2

➤ Evaluate the following areas of your life. Make a practical resolution for approaching each area in the fear of the Lord.

• Marriage

• Finances

• Career

• Entertainment

➤ Write a note to a man in your life who has displayed personal integrity. Thank him for his lifestyle and influence.

Read week 4 and complete the activities before the next group experience.

Day 1

Integrity

To become a better man, you align yourself under the comprehensive rule of God over every area of your life, embracing His kingdom agenda. You do it by choosing to be not just a man but a kingdom man. You do it by being the man David wrote about in my benchmark passage for manhood: Psalm 128.

No other passage in Scripture so comprehensively covers the kingdom impact of a kingdom man through four major spheres of life: personal, family, church, and community. This psalm was written specifically for men who want to follow the ways of the Lord. It's the anthem of a kingdom man.

Read Psalm 128.

How happy is everyone who fears the Lord,
who walks in His ways!
You will surely eat
what your hands have worked for.
You will be happy,
and it will go well for you.
Your wife will be like a fruitful vine
within your house,
your sons, like young olive trees
around your table.
In this very way
the man who fears the Lord
will be blessed.
May the Lord *bless you from Zion,*
so that you will see the prosperity of Jerusalem

all the days of your life
and will see your children's children!
Peace be with Israel.

Which part of this psalm speaks most personally to you?

If you used this psalm as a prayer for your life, which part of the psalm would you focus on? Why?

This psalm begins with the personal life (vv. 1-2) of a kingdom man, describing someone who fears the Lord. Then it moves to a man's family life (vv. 3-4), the church (v. 5a), and his patriarchal legacy both at home and in his community (vv. 5b-6).

Yet first and foremost, blessing comes when a kingdom man fears the Lord and walks in His ways in his personal life. It always starts there, so this week we will consider the personal life of a kingdom man. First, a kingdom man loves and lives with true integrity before God.

Define *integrity* in your own words.

Why do you think living with integrity is often difficult for men?

If we looked up the word *integrity* in the dictionary, the first definition we'd find would be something like this: "adherence to moral and ethical principles; soundness of moral character; honesty."[1] If we apply that definition to a kingdom context, we see that integrity is an adherence to moral and ethical principles as set forth by Jesus Christ.

Integrity is an adherence to moral and ethical
principles as set forth by Jesus Christ.

However, if we stopped there, we might fool ourselves into thinking that keeping all the rules of the Bible equates to operating with integrity. But simply keeping all of the rules isn't enough. Integrity is aligning ourselves with the rule of God both inside and outside. It's not only an external obedience but also an internal love and passion that drive our obedience.

That's why the Pharisees, though great at external obedience, could never live with true integrity.

Read Jesus' description of the Pharisees in Luke 11:39-44.
What was Jesus' primary indictment of them?

The Pharisees were like a coffee mug that's clean on the outside but still bears the stains of liquid deep on the inside. True integrity is soundness of moral character that comes from the inside. That's why, above anything else, a man of integrity knows and lives by the truth of the gospel. In the gospel Jesus doesn't clean only the outside; He gives us a brand-new inside. The new inside loves obedience. It loves falling in line with God's kingdom standards. That love naturally results in obedience on the outside.

If you continued reading dictionary definitions of *integrity*, you'd come across another reference that's usually used when the word refers to an object, like the hull of a ship: "a sound, unimpaired, or perfect condition."[2]

The hull of a ship might not have any visible cracks, but that doesn't mean it has integrity. There could be internal hemorrhaging that undermines the external appearance. True integrity begins in the heart, and it makes a man complete. Not only does he act obedient, but he also *is* obedient.

Here's the tricky thing about true integrity: it's something only you and God really know. I can't see what's inside you. But you know who you are and what you do when you're alone. That's often the litmus test of integrity: Who are you and what do you do when no one's looking? Would the people closest to you be surprised to see who you are and what you do when no one is around? Living as a kingdom man begins with an evaluation of your personal integrity.

Ask the Holy Spirit to examine your heart as you rate yourself on the following components of integrity. Circle the number beside each criterion, with 1 being low and 5 being high.

Adherence to biblical moral and ethical principles 1 2 3 4 5

Honesty   1 2 3 4 5

Desire to please and obey God   1 2 3 4 5

Moral excellence in private as well as in public   1 2 3 4 5

Pray about your responses to these criteria of integrity. Ask God to correct your heart and to help you bring your behavior in line with His Word.

Day 2

Fear

A kingdom man lives with integrity. A kingdom man also fears the Lord.

Read Psalm 128:1.

> *How happy is everyone who fears the LORD,*
> *who walks in His ways!*

What do you think it means to fear the Lord?

The Hebrew word *yare,* translated into the English as *fear,* combines the concepts of both dread and awe. It means kingdom men fear the Lord when they take Him seriously.

Now that sounds easy enough, doesn't it? Maybe not.

Do you think most men, even men who go to church, really take God seriously? Explain your answer.

What kinds of actions demonstrate that a man takes God seriously?

What kinds of actions demonstrate that a man doesn't take God seriously?

We live in a day of casual Christianity. Men seem to be politely Christian by acknowledging God but not necessarily taking him seriously. They readily admit the core truths of the Christian faith: "God is real. I am a sinner. Jesus is the only way of salvation." But that's where it stops.

There's no action that proves the validity of this confession. If the total of your Christianity is acknowledging the previous statements, congratulations. Satan can do the same thing and live the same way you do. He too knows God is real. And he certainly knows he's a sinner. He even knows Jesus is the only way of salvation. James 2:19 says, "You believe that God is one; you do well. The demons also believe—and they shudder." James argued that there has to be evidence that someone is truly a believer.

You know you don't really take God seriously when your faith makes almost no difference in your everyday life. But because a kingdom man fears God, he acknowledges and welcomes God's presence in every area of his life.

Because a kingdom man fears God, he acknowledges and welcomes God's presence in every area of his life.

Check the areas of your life in which you welcome and honor God's presence and rule.

☒ **Marriage and family**　　　　☒ **Church**
☒ **Career**　　　　　　　　　　☒ **Ministry**
☒ **Social life**　　　　　　　　☒ **Hobbies and entertainment**
☐ **Other:**

God is not just omnipresent, meaning He is everywhere at all times. He is also omniscient, meaning He knows everything at all times as well. God isn't just around when you're at church, having your devotions, and praying. Living life in the fear of God is a mind-set that takes Him seriously at all times and in all ways. Living in the fear of God means taking Him seriously by walking in His ways.

Read Proverbs 1:7.

> *The fear of the* Lord
> *is the beginning of knowledge;*
> *fools despise wisdom and discipline.*

Why is the fear of the Lord the beginning of wisdom?

Kingdom men don't take God lightly. They know the promises of God are true, whether they promise to bless or to judge. They know God means what He says, so His Word is to be obeyed. That kind of fear affects your thoughts, the way you use your time, what you say, and how you treat your family. To fear God means acknowledging Him as the Lord of your life and aligning your actions, words, and thoughts with His Word.

In God's kingdom rule, living in fear of Him means taking Him seriously by walking in His ways. It means taking God seriously with your feet, not just your feelings. It means more than a warm, fuzzy emotion you might experience on a Sunday morning or during a quiet time with God. While those things are great, they're not the test of your fear. Feelings fluctuate. They can change between the time you leave the sanctuary and get in your car. The proof that you fear God shows in your actions rather than in your emotions. It shows in whether you obey God's Word, aligning your life with His guidelines and principles instead of your own.

Check any evidence that you are living in fear of the Lord.

☐ I take God's Word seriously by reading and obeying it.

☐ I seek to align my life with God's will.

☐ I seek to grow in Christlike character and conduct.

☐ I view God with a healthy sense of dread and awe that leads me to genuine worship.

☐ I put God's kingdom first.

☐ I use my time, money, and resources to advance the kingdom.

☐ I testify to Christ's lordship through words and deeds.

☐ Other:

Do you fear the Lord, or do you think of Him as a kind, grandfatherly type who dispenses good advice but really doesn't understand the world you're living in? If it's more like the second, beware: God is not to be taken lightly.

Pray for a sense of awe in your spiritual life. Pray that you will see God more clearly as King and that you will respond in submission and loving obedience.

Day 3
Obedience

A kingdom man's personal life is lived with integrity. It's dominated by a fear of the Lord. And it's actualized through obedience in every area of his life. The life of a kingdom man can't be just mostly obedient or obedient only with the big things. As Jesus said, following Him requires a complete surrender of ourselves in obedience to Him: "If anyone wants to come with Me, he must deny himself, take up his cross, and follow Me. For whoever wants to save his life will lose it, but whoever loses his life because of Me will find it" (Matt. 16:24-25).

In your own words, what does it mean to deny yourself?

The Greek word for *life* that Jesus chose is *psyche,* which literally means *the vital force of life; a living soul.* Your soul is you. It's the core of who you are, as well as what makes you different from anyone else around you. Your soul is not your body but your will: your capacity to feel, think, choose, and desire. It's your very essence—the part of you that will continue beyond time into eternity. That's what Jesus asked you to surrender to Him.

Jesus said if you want to follow Him and thereby save your soul, you must do three things. First of all, you need to say no to yourself; that's what denying yourself is all about. It's necessary to deny yourself because your biggest problem in your relationship with Jesus is not outside you; your biggest problem is *you.* To follow Christ means you need to learn how to say no to you. In my case it's easy enough for me to say no to me when it comes to eating squash. But when it comes to eating fried chicken, it's a different story.

Identify some things you need to deny in order to follow Jesus.

Go back and draw an *X* through the ones you will commit to deny for Jesus' sake.

When you want something, you don't like to tell yourself no. Yet to fear God as King and follow Christ as your Master, you must deny yourself.

Second, you must take up your cross. This is a frequently misunderstood concept.

In your own words, what does it mean to take up your cross?

I often hear people quote this passage in relation to a difficult situation at work, at home, or in their personal lives. I hear things like "I'll just have to pick up my cross and put up with that person," "My in-law is the cross I must bear," or "I have a headache, so that must be my cross." But Jesus said you are to pick up *your* cross. The cross you are asked to bear is *you*. In Jesus' day there was only one reason the Roman government ordered someone to carry his own cross: he was going to be crucified on it. A cross is an instrument of death. Carrying a cross was an open, tangible submission to the law of the land—the Roman government.

When a believer denies himself and carries his cross, he submits to another law higher than himself. He yields himself to what God has asked of him: to deny his wants, desires, and will in exchange for following the wants, desire, and will of the One he's following. Even in the garden before Jesus carried His cross, He told God He didn't want to do it. But He also said, "Not My will, but Yours, be done" (Luke 22:42). To carry your cross is to yield your will fully to God's.

Check any past desires you had to give up in order to follow Christ.

☒ Ambition
☒ Status
☒ Materialism/wealth
☐ Other:

☒ Need to dominate
☒ Selfishness
☒ Self-image

Third, after denying yourself and taking up your cross, Jesus said to follow Him. But keep in mind where Jesus was going: He was on His way to die. To follow Him, then, is to put to death any parts of you that aren't fully submitted and obedient to the rule of Jesus. Paul said it this way: "Put to death what belongs to your worldly nature: sexual immorality, impurity, lust, evil desire, and greed, which is idolatry" (Col. 3:5).

> **Why do you think Paul said to "put to death" instead of "stop"? Why the violent language?**

We must not show mercy to the parts of us that aren't aligned with Jesus. We must ruthlessly put them to death, sometimes over and over again. The good news is that we're not alone in this fight. God is working in us for this same purpose. When we choose to crucify our sinful nature, we're embracing the work of the Holy Spirit in our lives.

Kingdom men are in a constant process of transformation into the likeness of Jesus. When they sense the old ways of their sinful nature rising up, they aggressively put them to death and progressively move forward in obedience to Christ.

> *Kingdom men are in a constant process of transformation into the likeness of Jesus.*

> **What expressions of the old sinful nature do you still struggle with?**

> **How are these sins affecting your obedience to Jesus?**

Confess any persistent sins to God. Accept Jesus' forgiveness, and by the power of the Spirit, put those old ways to death again.

Day 4

A Blessed Life

A kingdom man orders and aligns his personal world under the complete, comprehensive rule of Jesus. That means he walks with integrity as he fears the Lord and is committed to absolute obedience to his King. Psalm 128 tells us a man who does this will be blessed.

Read Psalm 128:1-2.

> *How happy is everyone who fears the LORD,*
> *who walks in His ways!*
> *You will surely eat*
> *what your hands have worked for.*
> *You will be happy,*
> *and it will go well for you.*

The same Hebrew word translated *happy* can also be translated *blessed*. What do you think it means to be blessed?

What specific elements in your life cause you to think you are blessed?

In Scripture a blessing refers to the favor and goodness of God. Psalm 128 says you'll be blessed if you fear the Lord and walk in His ways. The psalm goes on to outline three areas of your life in which you'll benefit if you fear the Lord and commit yourself to a life of obedience and integrity: your fortune, your feelings, and your future.

By functioning under the rule of God,

> *you will surely eat*
> *what your hands have worked for.*
> *Psalm 128:2*

In other words, you will have the capacity to enjoy your fortune, the benefits of your labor.

Is this a promise that those who fear the Lord will be rich?
What does this promise indicate?

Obeying God because you think He will reward you with material benefits isn't the kind of obedience God is looking for. In fact, it's not obedience at all, because it doesn't derive from a heart of love. It springs instead from a heart of greed. So this verse isn't a promise for health and wealth in exchange for righteous living. Instead, it's a recognition that God blesses those who work hard with integrity. If you demonstrate that kind of work ethic in your daily life, you'll have what you need to live. God will provide for you in a way that allows you to care for yourself, your family, and others around you. The Lord will bless you by providing for your material needs.

How have you seen God provide for your material needs in the past?

Verse 2 also says, "You will be happy." This refers to your feelings, but again, there needs to be some qualification. God doesn't exist to make you happy. He's not your cosmic butler, making sure all of your creature comforts are provided for. Rather, a kingdom man who fears the Lord understands the true source of happiness: God Himself.

> *A kingdom man who fears the Lord understands*
> *the true source of happiness: God Himself.*

God is the fountain of living water. He's the source of all real pleasure. And when you align yourself under His rule, you'll be a happy man, not because every situation in your life is perfect but because you're at peace with God.

Identify any areas of your life in which you are discontented.

How would placing your focus on God change the way you feel about the unsatisfying areas of your life?

Finally, if you fear God and walk in His ways, the psalm says, "It will go well for you" (v. 2). This is a statement about your future.

Are you prone to worry about the future? What specifically concerns you?

A kingdom man knows the truth of the saying "There is a God, and I'm not He." You aren't the one who controls the future. Many things are completely out of your control. But the good news for those who fear the Lord is that not only do you know the One who controls the future, but you also know He loves you and will take care of you. Just as God has provided for you in the past and is providing for you in the present, you can be confident of His provision for the future.

A kingdom man works hard at obedience, enjoys the benefit of that work, finds happiness in the Lord, and fully trusts the Lord with His future. That's a blessed life.

Thank God for the marks of His blessing in your life. Express your trust in Him to provide for your fortune, your feelings, and your future.

Day 5

Continuing the Blessing

God has laid down principles by which men can arrange their lives. If more men would abide by this kingdom order, the world would be drastically different. This is another dimension of being blessed.

In Scripture blessing refers to the favor and goodness God has designed to flow to you. But that's only one side of the blessing. God's blessings aren't just meant to flow *to* you; they're meant to flow *through* you. If you think God's blessing you entirely for your sake, you're missing half of the biblical principle.

Read the account of God's pronouncement of blessing on Abram.

The Lord said to Abram: "Go out from your land, your relatives,
and your father's house to the land that I will show you.
I will make you into a great nation, I will bless you, I will make
your name great and you will be a blessing. I will bless those
who bless you, I will curse those who treat you with contempt,
and all the peoples on earth will be blessed through you."
Genesis 12:1-3

List specific ways God would bless Abram.

What did God intend as the result of His blessing of Abram?

The story of Abram is a great model for God's blessing in the life of a kingdom man. In these verses you see some incredible promises from God to this man: to make him into a great nation, to make his name great, and even to bring him to a new land. But the result of this blessing was that Abram would be a conduit of God's blessing. He was blessed in order to be a blessing to others.

Read Galatians 3:6-9.

Just as Abraham believed God, and it was credited to him for righteousness, then understand that those who have faith are Abraham's sons. Now the Scripture saw in advance that God would justify the Gentiles by faith and told the good news ahead of time to Abraham, saying, All the nations will be blessed through you. So those who have faith are blessed with Abraham, who had faith.

How would God's blessing of Abraham eventually be fulfilled?

There's a disconnect in God's kingdom system of blessing when men think blessings stop with them. God isn't blessing you so that you can be blessed. He's blessing you for the sake of others in your sphere of influence. When God blessed Abram, the ultimate end of that blessing was that all nations of the earth would be blessed with the knowledge of the gospel of Jesus Christ.

There's a disconnect in God's kingdom system of blessing when men think blessings stop with them.

Similarly, God has blessed you as a kingdom man. But always keep in mind that you aren't being blessed for your own benefit. One practical way we see this principle in Scripture is through the true purpose of work.

Read Ephesians 4:28.

The thief must no longer steal. Instead, he must do honest work with his own hands, so that he has something to share with anyone in need.

What is the purpose of work, according to this verse?

If you think you're working to earn enough money to buy a big house, drive a nice car, and live in luxury, think again. You're working in order to be a blessing to others. This is how life in the kingdom works, but to embrace this principle requires a drastic change in mind-set.

List some ways God has blessed you. Beside each blessing write one way you are using it to bless others. If you are not blessing others, write ways you could be a conduit of God's blessings.

If you allow yourself to be a conduit rather than a cul-de-sac for blessings, God can use you to bless others. In fact, when you ask God to do something for you, always request that this blessing will flow through you to others. When you do this, you align yourself with God's purpose of benefiting others through His blessing to you.

A kingdom man lives in fear of the Lord. He lives a life of integrity and obedience. And when you walk in God's ways, you'll be blessed, not only for your own sake but also for the blessing of those around you. In these ways a kingdom man's personal life is the beginning of a better world.

Pray about ways you can pass on God's blessings to those around you. Pray about material blessings as well as talents, influence, and ministry.

1. *http://dictionary.reference.com/browse/integrity.*
2. Ibid.

The Home of a
KINGDOM
MAN

A man's decision to marry a woman and begin a family is one of the most important decisions he will ever make. It ought to come only after great thought and preparation, although these steps frequently don't take place. I have two daughters, both of whom are married. When the time came for them to get married, their future husbands had to do a lot more than ask me for permission to marry them. These were my princesses, and I wasn't about to hand them over to just anyone.

In fact, part of the process of winning an Evans woman involved writing me a detailed, lengthy letter stating everything he would be responsible to do and be as the husband of my daughter. Then I filed it away in case I ever needed to remind them what they had committed to do.

Marriage is a serious commitment and should be entered only when both parties fully comprehend its meaning and purpose.

When a man is a successful husband and father, it not only brings blessing to his own life but enables his wife and family to fulfill their divine destinies as well.

WEEK FIVE
Group Experience

Get Started

1. Share one insight you gained as you completed week 4.

2. Why do you think living with integrity is difficult for men?

3. How would you describe to a younger man what a life of integrity looks like?

4. Why does a fear of the Lord lead to a life of integrity? Why does it lead to a life of blessing?

Man Up

Watch the video teaching for session 5 as you complete the viewer guide below.

To access the teaching sessions, use the instructions in the back of your Bible study book.

Nothing demonstrates the decline of our world like the _____ of the family.

You are to be a kingdom man at _____ first.

When a woman is left out of the kingdom equation, you limit or even cancel God's _____ with you.

God created the family to _____ His rule in history.

A _____ is a spiritually binding relationship brought about by God, over which God rules.

When a man becomes a kingdom man and he fears God, _____ will begin to occur in his wife.

When you create a stable environment based on your fear of God, your wife becomes _____, and she will begin to _____.

A man should be his wife's _____.

There is a _____ to being a savior.

A man is to be his wife's _____.

Sanctification is taking somebody from where they _____ and turning them into what they ought to _____.

A man is to oversee his wife's _____.

Spiritual change takes place as a kingdom man uses kingdom principles, with God at the top, _____ in his wife.

A man is to be his wife's _____.

Think about _____ every time you think about _____, so it's never only about you.

When your wife discovers that she is necessary, you get to have _____.

Our children's roots don't run deep because no one is _____ them.

The father is not in the home setting the _____, the _____ _____, the rights and wrongs for the children.

The _____ is the place for kingdom men to take charge.

Whoever owns the _____ owns the _____.

Our families are being _____ because kingdom men aren't leading them.

Discuss the video teaching with your group, using the questions below.

1. What words would your family use to describe you? How do you wish they would describe you?

2. What are you doing to oversee your wife's spiritual change and development? What should you be doing?

3. What are some practical ways you can serve your wife and children?

4. What might need to change in your schedule so that you can lead from the table?

5. What specifically can the men in your group pray for your wife and children?

Close with prayer.

Hit the Streets

Scripture Memory

Your wife will be like a fruitful vine
within your house,
your sons, like young olive trees
around your table. Psalm 128:3

➤ Choose one unexpected way to serve your wife this week.

➤ Engage each of your children in a one-to-one conversation about what is happening in his or her life.

Read week 5 and complete the activities before the next group experience.

Day 1

The Power of the Home

Very few problems exist in our culture today that can't be directly traced to the family. That's not to say bad things would never happen if we got our families in order, but I believe we could take a significant chunk out of crime, poverty, sexual transgression, and many other societal ills if the family functioned as God intended.

Do you agree with the previous statements? Why or why not?

Read Genesis 1:26-28. How do you think God's command to "be fruitful, multiply, fill the earth, and subdue it" is related to being created in the image of God?

Because humankind was created in the image of God, filling the earth with other humans would mean filling the earth with fellow image bearers. The goal of the family isn't just to have a happy place to call home. It's to spread the image of God throughout the world.

The family, when seen from a kingdom perspective, is God's means of spreading His kingdom and rule throughout history. That's why Satan is intent on destroying the family. If he can destroy the family, he can destroy the future expansion of God's kingdom rule. Whoever owns the family owns the future.

Whoever owns the family owns the future.

How did your family of origin influence your development as a kingdom man, both positively and negatively?

What specifically would change about the way you interact with your current family if you began seeing it as the means by which God spreads His kingdom?

Take a look around you, and you'll see how Satan is trying to redefine the family. It's not just about whether marriage is defined as one woman with one man. Nor is it about parenting styles and techniques. It's about the order God instituted at creation and our alignment under His kingship. In redefining the family, Satan is attempting to set up a rival kingdom that seeks to undermine God's purpose for the home.

What effects do you see of Satan's efforts to redefine the family?

In warping society's view of manhood, Satan's doing the same thing he tried to do when he used Herod to kill the baby boys after Jesus was born. Satan was attempting to destroy the future. Because your role as a kingdom man is critical, Satan's goal is to keep you from performing it according to God's kingdom principles.

Are you feeling the weight of your responsibility for your family? I hope so. It's your job to lead your family to understand, love, and embrace the values of the kingdom of God. There is no higher calling. It eclipses your calling at work, in the community, and even at church. Your primary responsibility is to your family, and a significant way you can put your family first is in the way you spend your time.

> *It's your job to lead your family to understand, love,*
> *and embrace the values of the kingdom of God.*

In a typical week how much time do you intentionally spend with your family?

Honestly rank your priorities in life, after God, by numbering the following activities from 1 (highest priority) to 11 (lowest priority).

☒ ___ Entertainment   ☒ ___ Education
☒ ___ Marriage and family   ☒ ___ Exercise
☒ ___ Home improvement   ☒ ___ Church
☒ ___ Ministry and witnessing ☒ ___ Sports
☒ ___ Hobbies   ☒ ___ Career
☒ ___ Relationship with God

Go back and check one pursuit you must limit to create more quality time with your family.

If you believe in the importance of the family, it will show up in your schedule. You must intentionally make yourself a consistent part of the family. Many men simply pop in on special occasions and then consume themselves with their work and leisure, leaving the hearts of their wives and children empty. Nothing can fill the void created by the absence of a husband or a father. It doesn't have to be fancy, and it doesn't have to be formal, but it does have to be a priority.

The time you spend with your family should never be a second thought. It should always be your first thought. Put first things first. If you haven't done it in the past, it's never too late to start.

> **What is one thing you will do this week to begin or increase intentional time with your family?**

Bringing the family together for breakfast or dinner each day might not seem like much, but it's a start. Your family might even fight you over that decision. But simple decisions like this will pay big dividends in the future. Make the choice today. Be present. Be a leader. Be a kingdom man for your family.

Pray that God will give you clarity and insight to know what to limit in your schedule for the sake of your family, as well as perseverance to follow through. Then prayerfully implement those changes.

Day 2

The Covenant of Marriage

The two main components of the family are marriage and parenting. Messed-up marriages lead to messed-up parenting. Although good marriages don't necessarily result in good parenting, they certainly start you in the right direction.

Marriage, in God's design, isn't simply a means of love and happiness. While those things are important, they aren't the most important things a marriage is designed to produce. Marriage is a covenant union designed by God to equip both partners to carry out their divine purpose of advancing God's kingdom.

Carefully examine the definition of *marriage* in the previous sentence. Underline the part of the definition that least resembles the way most people look at marriage today.

Specifically, how is your marriage increasing your capacity as a couple to advance the kingdom?

A covenant is more than an agreement or a contract. In terms of marriage, one of the key components of a covenant that's been lost in our day of quickie divorces is the seriousness of that covenant.

We see in the Book of Malachi that when marriage is broken, so is fellowship with God. In the days of Malachi, the people of Judah were wondering why God wasn't responding even though they were crying on the altar and offering sacrifices. Malachi said God's silence stemmed from their casual treatment of marriage: "Because the LORD has been a witness between you and the wife of your youth. You have acted treacherously against her, though she was your marriage partner and your wife by covenant" (Mal. 2:14).

In a similar way, Peter taught the early believers to take marriage as seriously as God takes it. He admonished husbands to honor their wives "as co-heirs of the grace of life, so that your prayers will not be hindered" (1 Pet. 3:7). God takes the covenant of marriage so seriously that He links fellowship with Him to fellowship between a husband and wife. To break one covenant is to break the other.

> How do you know when people take marriage as seriously as God does?

> What about you? How seriously do you take your marriage? Give evidence for your answer.

When you approach your marriage as a covenant, with fear of and reverence for God, Psalm 128 says, "Your wife will be like a fruitful vine" (v. 3).

> Why do you think the wife of a kingdom man is compared to a fruitful vine?

If you've ever been to a vineyard or seen the way grapes grow, you understand that grapes can't survive without help. Because they grow on a vine, they need a structure to climb on and cling to. There must be a post, a fence, or a wall—something stable that gives balance and support. Otherwise, the vine will drag on the ground and die because it won't be able to absorb sunlight.

If the wife of a kingdom man is like a fruitful vine, the kingdom man himself is what the vine clings to. Your job is to provide strength, stability, and support so that your wife can thrive and grow. If your wife is to be the kingdom woman she was created to be, you must provide for her a place of security that is strong and stable so that she can cling to you and will want to. By enabling and encouraging her to cling to you, you will discourage her from clinging to something else.

> *Your job is to provide strength, stability, and support*
> *so that your wife can thrive and grow.*

Can your wife count on you to do the things you say you will do? Give evidence for your answer.

Provide some examples of ways you can create a safe, secure environment in which your wife can flourish.

Your wife needs to know that she can trust you. That you are dependable. That you are willing to make hard choices for the good of your family. She needs to know that you'll take an active role to sustain your romantic relationship and to parent your children. That's how you become a man she can cling to. It's by proving over and over again that you're a stable, wise ruler of your domain.

When you do that, you will begin to see your wife begin to blossom. She will be free to become who she was created to be, and she will indeed, like a vine, produce great fruit.

Is your wife producing the kind of kingdom fruit she ought to be? If not, maybe you're not being the kind of stable structure she can cling to.

Pray for your wife, specifically the challenges and opportunities you know she will have today. Ask God to show you ways to provide a safe, stable environment for her.

Day 3

A Husband's Responsibility

In God's design for the covenant of marriage, a husband serves as the stable force that allows his wife to grow and flourish. That's the responsibility of a kingdom man. Up until now we've studied much about your domain, rule, and authority. All of that is true. But none of those truths should lead you to believe your wife's job is to wait on you. In fact, the opposite is true.

Read Ephesians 5:22-32. Describe a husband's role in marriage.

Describe a wife's role in marriage.

According to this passage, who do you think has the most difficult job in marriage, the husband or the wife? Explain your answer.

It's hard to imagine a higher calling for husbands than what Paul described. A kingdom man loves his wife as Christ loved the church. And how did Christ love the church? Last time I checked, Christ loved the church to death. He was willing to sacrifice everything for her salvation.

How many marriages would change if men began to truly love their wives sacrificially? What if men began sacrificing time they would spend watching sports and instead went for a walk? What would happen if men started sacrificing their evenings so that their wives could have time away from the house and a break from the kids? What would happen if men started sacrificing simple things, like the choice of a movie or the type of dinner, just because they loved their wives? Big things would happen.

What small thing can you sacrifice today to show your love for your wife?

You might argue, "But I'm a man. I'm no weakling or pushover. I'm in charge of my house. What I say goes, and if I do what you're saying, my wife will treat me like a doormat." Is that what you really think? Do you think Jesus' death on the cross was a display of weakness? I don't think so. Jesus was a man's man. It was precisely because of His strength that He was willing to silently subject Himself to the punishment and pain of the crucifixion.

Paul said a man should not only love his wife sacrificially but should also aid in her spiritual development. In this way men are meant to play a role in the sanctification of their wives. To sanctify something means to set it apart as special and unique. It means to make it holy. A man helps in his wife's sanctification by leading her in discipleship and encouraging her to grow into the daughter of God she was made to be.

A man helps in his wife's sanctification by leading her in discipleship and encouraging her to grow into the daughter of God she was made to be.

This process looks different for every person and is complicated by issues of past failure, sin, and pain. For a husband to take an active role in his wife's spiritual growth, he must be a student of his wife. He must truly know her.

How can being a student of your wife help you know how
to encourage and facilitate her spiritual growth?

How are you involved in your wife's spiritual growth?

When you're a student of your wife, you know how to pray for her. You learn her specific needs, dreams, fears, and insecurities. You equip yourself to love her well, as a kingdom man should (see Eph. 5:25). You prepare yourself to love your wife like your own body (see Eph. 5:28).

Whatever you do for yourself you ought to do for your wife. You are to treat her with the care you treat your own body. You're to think in terms of two, never in terms of one. If you love your wife like this, she will never have trouble living up to her responsibility in the marriage or submitting to your leadership.

Express in your own words what it means to love your wife like your
own body. Give examples of ways you would express this.

One more thing: your marriage isn't just about you. It's not just about her. It's about the gospel. Paul said in Ephesians 5:32, "This mystery is profound, but I am talking about Christ and the church." When you love your wife like this and she willingly submits to you, your marriage becomes a walking, talking, living, breathing illustration of the gospel.

In what ways do you think marriage can illustrate the gospel?

People should be able to look at the marriage of a kingdom man and see a representation of the gospel: a living picture of self-giving, sacrificial love on your part and voluntary submission on her part. It's a high calling but one that kingdom men need to embrace, not just for our sakes but for the sakes of all those around us.

Express to God your willingness to be a kingdom man in your marriage by loving your wife sacrificially. Pray that He will make your marriage a representation of the gospel.

Day 4

Raising Olive Trees

There's a progression in Psalm 128. It moves from integrity in a kingdom man's personal life, then in his marriage, and finally with his children. When you fear the Lord and walk in His ways and when your wife is a fruitful vine in your home, your children will be "like young olive trees around your table" (v. 3).

> Write one word that describes your relationship with your children. Why did you choose that word?

> What one word would you use to describe your wife's relationship with your children? Why did you choose that word?

To grasp the fullness of the promise in these verses, you have to know something about olive trees. Notice that verse doesn't say the kids will be olive trees but young olive trees. That's because an olive tree takes 15 or more years to fully develop.

If an olive plant is nurtured correctly, it will become an olive tree that can produce olives for more than two thousand years. When I was at the garden of Gethsemane in Israel, I saw two-thousand-year-old olive trees that were still producing olives. These olive trees are still around and still productive because during their formative years, care was taken to develop very deep root systems. Psalm 128 therefore pictures a household in which children grow up and pass along the kingdom principles they learned from one generation to another. How, then, can a kingdom man parent in such a way as to pass on a heritage of faith to his children? What can he do to cultivate deep roots in his children?

One of the greatest things you can offer your children as a kingdom man is to be a model of an olive tree with deep roots of stability.

Read Psalm 1. What are some ways this psalm defines stability?

Why do you think seeing stability in the father would be important to a child's development?

Do you think your children see you as stable in terms of modeling a kingdom agenda? Why or why not?

We live in days of constant change and motion. It's evident not only in technological advancement but also in relationships, marriages, and finances. With everything in motion, one of the greatest gifts we can give our children is stability.

> *With everything in motion, one of the greatest gifts*
> *we can give our children is stability.*

No matter what else is happening in the world, the children of a kingdom man can be confident of having stability at home. That stability fuels them to take on the world in flux around them. Establishing this kind of stability isn't that difficult. You do it by providing for your kids' needs. You do it by talking with them about their days at school. But most of all, you do it by simply being there—fully present, not just in body but in mind and heart too. That's why Psalm 128 pictures these young olive trees around a table.

A table is a great place to exercise leadership. A Jewish father raised his family around the table. The table wasn't just a place for eating; it was a place for nurturing. Food was simply the context for discipleship and relationship building. When a Jewish father sat around the table, he wasn't just filling his stomach. He was convening the family there to lead. If we choose to view the table in the same way, think about all that might happen there. It's at the table where the family is led in devotions. It's there where a father hears of any behavioral concerns. It's there that he hands out work responsibilities and checks on whether assigned chores have been completed. It's there that educational issues are discussed and strategies are established for achieving goals. It's around the table that a father learns what peer groups his children are associating with and what information they are putting into their minds. It's there that a father pours value and significance into the lives of his children by consistently listening to them and spending time with them.

A Jewish family didn't sit at the table for 20 minutes. The father spent several hours there each day teaching, listening to, knowing, and leading his family. These things were done at other times as well, but those occasions were always in addition to time spent at the table. This is because fruitful vines and olive trees need consistent nurturing to grow and produce.

Yet so many of our tables sit empty today. Men's schedules are full. Children's schedules are full. In failing to prioritize the consistency of time spent at the table or other daily family times, we have failed to lead our families well. As a result, a generation of young people have conformed their consciences to the culture rather than to the truth of God's Word, lovingly and diligently imparted at the table.

How often do you eat a meal with your entire family?

In what ways are you currently teaching, guiding, and connecting with your children?

What kinds of discussions would you like to have with your children?

It's through places like the table that stability is established for children. The table is where a kingdom man intentionally relates to those he has been entrusted to lead. Wherever you carry out the functions of the table, don't neglect this critical responsibility of being a father.

Pray specifically for the time you will spend with your family today. Pray that God will help you facilitate good conversation and intimate communication with your family, either through spontaneous times or planned occasions like those at the family table.

Day 5

Bring Them Up

A kingdom man plays games with his kids. A kingdom man tells stories and listens to his children's stories. A kingdom man drives his kids to school, shows up at baseball practice, and enjoys tea parties. These may seem like small things, but they build an environment of love and stability for your children. And though small at the time, they eventually add up to something big.

But in order to see any of those things happen, a kingdom man has to make intentional choices. Paul mentioned some of those choices in Ephesians 6:4: "Fathers, don't stir up anger in your children, but bring them up in the training and instruction of the Lord."

What are some ways a father might stir up anger in his children?

Do you think your father lived by these words? Explain your answer.

What were some of the effects of his decisions on your life?

Do you find yourself following your father's example in making decisions? If so, how?

You know how it is. You spend all day at work. You are physically, emotionally, and mentally tired. You want to do nothing else except sit in your chair, read your newspaper or computer screen, or watch TV. And then here come the children. It might be easy to respond in anger at a time like this.

Stirring up anger in your children doesn't always involve physical or verbal abuse; it often happens in more subtle ways. If your kids sense you are too busy or too tired for them, anger and resentment slowly begin to burn in their hearts, eventually working themselves out in rebellion. Or if you constantly push your children toward activities you enjoyed but they don't prefer, you are inciting their anger. You might not see the immediate effects of that anger, but these actions will not help you raise olive trees that will produce fruit for the kingdom long into the future.

Identify any ways you could be stirring up anger in your children.

What practical steps can you take to reverse this tendency?

Paul said instead of stirring up anger, we should bring up children in the training and instruction of the Lord. To Paul, the opposite of stirring up anger in kids is to teach them about the Lord. This isn't restricted to teaching them the Bible or taking them to Sunday School. Instruction about the Lord encompasses the entire way we deal with our children, helping them realize that God's ways are their guide for every aspect of their lives. As kingdom men, we need to actively and intentionally parent our children the way God parents us.

As kingdom men, we need to actively and intentionally parent our children the way God parents us.

Name things you are doing to instruct your children in the ways of the Lord.

What are three characteristics of the way God parents us as our Father?

1.

2.

3.

There are many ways we might describe God's fatherhood. He's certainly patient with us. He's also affectionate. He values and desires quality time. He's interested in the smallest details of our lives. He's consistent in His expectations and discipline.

All of these characteristics are filtered through His love. There is no action toward us as Christians that's not rooted in and motivated by our Father's love. Even when He disciplines us, He does so with our good in mind. Whereas we might discipline our kids from anger, frustration, or retribution, God never does. He is always loving in His discipline.

Can you recall a time when you disciplined your children from anger? How could you have expressed loving discipline in that situation?

There's nothing like love to take the steam out of anger. To bring our children up in the Lord, as God has brought us up, is to be motivated always by love. That may mean the next time you get angry or frustrated, you need to step away and take some deep breaths. It might mean you don't need to take every situation seriously. It might mean you need to stop taking yourself seriously so that you can act silly with your kids.

In each of these cases, the way you respond in love is by reminding yourself what God has done for you in Christ. Pause, remember your loving Father, and then commit to emulate His example in your particular situation. If you do that, you'll go a long way in introducing your kids to God's kingdom ways.

Identify any areas of parenting in which you need to improve.

☐ Spending time with your kids

☐ Disciplining in love

☐ Showing love in the way you talk and relate to your kids

☐ Encouraging your kids

☐ Deliberately teaching your kids about the Lord

☐ Other:

Circle an area you will work on immediately.

Thank God for His perfect fatherhood. Ask Him for help with specific areas of your parenting that are falling short of His example.

The Influence of a
KINGDOM
MAN

Closing in on my fourth decade of ministry, I'm becoming increasingly aware of the brevity of life. No one is guaranteed another day on earth. With that awareness comes a narrowing of focus—a desire to make every moment count and to ensure that every choice brings glory to God and blessings to others.

Your destiny as a kingdom man isn't only to be different but also to make a difference. It's your responsibility to take your influence beyond the scope of your own home and into the world. Kingdom men go public.

Instead of running from responsibility as men in today's culture do, kingdom men are ready to step up to the plate and to be leaders in their churches and communities. No greater challenge exists today than the need to impact our communities and our country for Christ. Men who will take a stand for the kingdom of God are desperately needed in our nation and our world.

Change for good is possible if men will be kingdom men, abiding by the kingdom values set forth in Psalm 128.

We can make a difference if we are individually responsible, stay attentive to our families, assume leadership in our churches, and become influencers in our communities.

WEEK SIX
Group Experience

Get Started

1. Share one insight you gained as you completed week 5.

2. Why, from God's perspective, is the home such a powerful place?

3. What positive and negative effects of the home you grew up in can you see in your own life?

4. How do most men view their marriage and children? How should a kingdom man view his?

Man Up

Watch the video teaching for session 6 as you complete the viewer guide below.

To access the teaching sessions, use the instructions in the back of your Bible study book.

The _____ is a local manifestation of the kingdom of God.

It is inconceivable in the Bible that a kingdom man would not have a meaningful relationship with God's place of _____.

Zion referred to God's holy _____
_____, that special place set aside for God's unique presence.

The temple was where a father took his _____ to worship Yahweh.

God has localized, unique _____ that bring unique _____ attached to them.

Jesus established the _____ to rule in history.

The church legislates on earth on behalf of _____.

Satan wants to keep men _____ from the church.

The church draws down heaven to earth so that earth has a vehicle
for the _____ of God to be manifested.

God has always called _____ to lead in the church.

God calls men to be leaders because they are _____.

Men go to church for the collective _____ of God.

Men go to church for _____.

The goal of the church is to primarily disciple _____ because men
are responsible for discipling their _____.

The church is where men use their gifts, talents, and skills for the furtherance
of the _____.

Your wife is there to collaborate, not _____.

God is changing the culture by kingdom men, starting with themselves,
going to their homes, taking it to the church, and expanding it
into _____.

We're growing weak men in the culture because we're not developing them
in the _____ and then in the _____.

A kingdom man isn't measured by his title but by his _____.

God will raise up surrogate _____ for those without them.

The church is to mobilize its men to _____—in a righteous way—
as a representative of the King.

Discuss the video teaching with your group, using the questions below.

1. How should a kingdom man view the local church?

2. To what specific involvement in your church do you think God is calling you?

3. How do you think the community should view local churches?

4. How can you personally be involved in impacting the community for the kingdom of God?

5. What is one specific action God is calling you to take in response to this study?

Close with prayer.

Hit the Streets

Scripture Memory

May the LORD bless you from Zion,
so that you will see the prosperity of Jerusalem
all the days of your life. Psalm 128:5

➤ Do you have a spiritual father and a spiritual son in your local church? If not, begin to identify a man whom you can influence and a man who can influence you.

➤ Embrace your destiny of leadership and consider leading another Bible-study group through *Kingdom Man*.

Read week 6 and complete the activities to conclude your study of *Kingdom Man*.

Day 1

An Ambassador for the Kingdom

We've been examining Psalm 128 to discover the values and priorities of a kingdom man. When a man fears the Lord, aligning himself under God, the results will spread outward to influence his family, his church, and his community.

Read Psalm 128 once more.

> *How happy is everyone who fears the Lord,*
> *who walks in His ways!*
> *You will surely eat*
> *what your hands have worked for.*
> *You will be happy,*
> *and it will go well for you.*
> *Your wife will be like a fruitful vine*
> *within your house,*
> *your sons, like young olive trees*
> *around your table.*
> *In this very way*
> *the man who fears the Lord*
> *will be blessed.*
> *May the Lord bless you from Zion,*
> *so that you will see the prosperity of Jerusalem*
> *all the days of your life*
> *and will see your children's children!*
> *Peace be with Israel.*

135

In the previous Scripture, underline areas in which a kingdom man's relationship with God spreads outward.

How are you currently taking responsibility and assuming leadership to maximize your influence beyond your home?

A kingdom man can't be content to rule only his personal life under the lordship of Jesus. Neither can he stop at leading his family to live by kingdom principles. He must move further outward into the world at large to truly fulfill God's destiny for him. If you're a man in God's kingdom, you must accept the priorities of that kingdom. And God's priority is the advancement of His kingdom.

Read 2 Corinthians 5:17-21. What do you think it means for a kingdom man to be an ambassador for Christ?

Paul adopted kingdom-oriented language in this passage to describe a Christian's role in the world. All who have been reconciled to God are ambassadors. An ambassador is a citizen of one kingdom who lives in the middle of another in order to spread the values and culture of his homeland to the land where he now lives. Though an ambassador might be thousands of miles from his home, he isn't bound by the laws and regulations of his country of residence. He lives by the laws of his own land. While abroad, he intentionally seeks to live differently in order to represent his home kingdom, to which he owes his loyalty.

Unlike ambassadors to other countries, a kingdom man never stops being an ambassador. There's no down time, because no matter where you go, you don't change who you are. As a new creation in Christ, you are an ambassador in a foreign land.

To truly fulfill the purpose of a kingdom ambassador, you can't stay confined to your home. An ambassador is no good to his home country if he stays locked behind the gates of an embassy. In fact, the primary reason the person is in the foreign country is to move outside those gates and infiltrate the world around him.

In the same way, a kingdom man is meant to operate in the world. Go to work. Eat out. Coach sports teams. Go to the bank. You get the idea. But you are meant to do those things with a larger purpose in mind. When you begin to embrace your role as an ambassador, the motivation behind all of these ordinary activities changes. You're always looking for any opportunity to advance the kingdom you represent.

A kingdom man is meant to operate in the world.

How can a kingdom man be an ambassador in each of the following arenas?

Workplace:

Social circles:

Restaurants:

Schools:

Read Ephesians 5:15-16.

Pay careful attention, then, to how you walk—not as unwise people but as wise—making the most of the time, because the days are evil.

How might you remind yourself daily of the need to have a kingdom perspective as you go through life?

Two crucial areas where we must grasp the responsibility of being a kingdom man are the church and the community at large. Both of these areas desperately need kingdom men.

Are you up to the challenge?

Pray that God will make you attentive to opportunities this week to influence your church and community for the kingdom.

Day 2

Blessings from Zion

Psalm 128:5 says a kingdom man receives blessings from Zion. Scripture contains a number of references to this place. The mountain called Zion served as a holy place where God's presence could be found. There is also a city called Zion—the city of David, or Jerusalem, where God dwelled. The temple in Old Testament culture, the central place of worship for Israel, was also referred to as Zion. In essence, Zion was the place where the Israelites met to be reminded that they were a covenant people who thought alike, acted alike, and viewed life alike because they all lived under the same King and belonged to the same kingdom.

That sounds a lot like the church to me.

In your own words, what is the church?

Who is more involved in your church, men or women?
Why do you think that is true?

If an individual Christian is the ambassador, the church is the embassy. An embassy is a sovereign territory on foreign soil where the rules and laws of the representative nation apply. Embassies never belong to the countries in which they are located. They belong to the country they represent. If you visited another country as an American citizen and went to the American embassy, you would find that American laws and procedures were carried out there, no matter what country you were visiting. The American embassy is fundamentally a little bit of America a long way from home.

The church is supposed to be a little bit of heaven a long way from home, a place where the values of eternity are made manifest in history. The church is where anyone in any culture should be able to clearly observe what life is like in the kingdom of God.

How closely does your church match that description? Explain why you answered as you did.

How do you think most of your church's members view your church?

As an individual, you can experience God's power and blessing up to a certain extent. But God never intended for you to experience those things in isolation. Some aspects of God's blessing can come only from Zion—from a connection with the people of God.

When a kingdom man connects with the community of faith, he will get more out of his experience with God and will receive more of His blessings in his life than he would on his own.

A church is like a family. Each family member will experience certain things on his or her own. But other things, like a family vacation, occur only as a result of being connected to the group. In the Old Testament a man took his family and those under his care to Zion because there he knew each of them would receive favor and direction from God. There the principles and promises of the covenant would be transferred from one generation to another. There the man connected his family to something bigger than themselves—a community of people who thought and functioned according to God's kingdom covenant. Today when a kingdom man connects with the community of faith, he will get more out of his experience with God and will receive more of His blessings in his life than he would on his own.

Read Hebrews 10:24-25.

Let us be concerned about one another in order to promote love and good works, not staying away from our worship meetings, as some habitually do, but encouraging each other, and all the more as you see the day drawing near.

What are some ways you are being blessed and encouraged through involvement in your church?

How are you blessing others in your church?

Just as Satan seeks to break up the family in an effort to destroy the future, he also wants to break up the community of believers. Why? Because he knows an anemic church will never experience God's unique presence. That's where kingdom men can make a difference.

Many men come to church only because they are pressured to do so or because they are made to feel guilty for not doing so. They stand there with a nagging feeling that something just doesn't fit—kind of the way I would feel if my wife, Lois, asked me to hold her purse. Something just doesn't seem manly about church for many men. It's just too cute, with pretty decorations, soft music, long songs, and an atmosphere designed to evoke emotions. This is why a lot of men simply do their time, albeit sincerely, rather than view church as a vehicle through which they are to change the world.

Yet that wasn't the church Jesus established. He described the church as a force that even the gates of hell couldn't prevail against: "The forces of Hades will not overpower it" (Matt. 16:18). *Ecclesia*, or *church*, in New Testament Greek societies referred to a governing counsel that legislated on behalf of the population. It didn't refer to a place where men went to simply get inspired but to a place where they came together to exercise their rule.

Somewhere between the cross and contemporary culture, the concept of *ecclesia* has been watered down from the full potency of its original meaning. To be a part of the *ecclesia*, as Jesus stated it, was to participate in the governing body that He has empowered to bring heaven's point of view in hell's society. The church is intended to bring God's governance into the relevant application and practice of humankind.

Let's take some initiative. The church needs kingdom men, and it needs us now.

Pray for your pastor and church. Pray for a fresh vision in your congregation of how it can influence the world for God's kingdom.

Day 3

A Kingdom Man and His Church

In our world today many churches have strayed from their purpose, as heaven's embassy on earth, to more closely resemble a club. As a result, we are experiencing a cultural tsunami that is sweeping away a generation of men and boys, keeping them from becoming the kingdom men God intended them to be. Like an assembly line, the church was designed to produce kingdom men—visible, verbal, unapologetic disciples of Jesus. When an assembly line doesn't produce what it is supposed to produce, we can conclude there's a flaw in the factory that must be addressed. When we look at the weakness of Christian men today, we must also conclude there's a flaw in the factory that was established to produce them.

What do you think that flaw is in churches today? Why do you think they are failing to produce kingdom men?

What are a kingdom man's responsibilities in producing other kingdom men?

Read 1 Timothy 3:1-7. Record the leadership qualities you possess.

Paul carefully set forth a comprehensive list of qualities that church leaders should embody. Notice that all of these qualities are meant to be found in men.

People debate what exactly an overseer is. Some say it's the pastor; others claim it's a group of professional and lay pastors who lead together. But all agree that these verses describe the highest office in the church: the leaders. If the church is meant to be a visual demonstration of life in the kingdom, the way the church leadership is structured should reflect God's design in creation. That's why these leaders are men.

But in many churches, women are usually the ones who are most ready to step forward and lead. Men are content to sit and soak instead of assuming responsibility for the vision and direction of the body of Christ. If the church is going to progress forward in its mission to extend the kingdom of God, kingdom men must get off the couch, put down the video-game controls, roll up their sleeves, and get down to business.

Are you involved in any leadership role in your church?
☐ Yes ☐ No

If not, why not?

From your observation what areas of your church need leadership?

What would you have to rearrange in your life to be a leader in one of those areas?

Every man shouldn't be an overseer; every man can't be an overseer. But every man can be a spiritual father in the church. That's the kind of relationship Paul had with Timothy and Titus, and kingdom men can follow his example.

Paul called Timothy and Titus his true sons in the faith (see 1 Tim. 1:2; Titus 1:4). What qualities characterize that kind of relationship?

Is there anyone you look to as a spiritual father? What guidance does he provide?

Is there anyone who would consider you a spiritual father? What guidance are you providing?

In his letters to Timothy and Titus, Paul addressed men who were taking over pastoral responsibilities in first-century churches. While Paul was careful to tell them about preaching, teaching, and serving, he also talked to them about spiritual mentoring. In the same way a home is a place where parents rear their children to become responsible adults, the church exists to provide a parenting environment in which God's children can grow to be spiritually mature and responsible.

Today's church is missing spiritual fathers like Paul. Without spiritual fathers to provide examples, boys learn a feminized version of what it means to be a man, perhaps becoming nice and helpful rather than strong and responsible. Even though Timothy and Titus weren't Paul's biological children, he spoke to them and related to them as a father would to a son. It's bad enough if a young man doesn't have a biological father to mentor him and help him grow, but when there's no spiritual father as well, he's fatherless in two crucial respects.

The Word of God isn't simply to be known but also to be applied. When Jesus mentored His disciples, He imparted truth in ways that challenged them to apply it. Discipleship always includes information, but the discipleship process isn't complete without emulation. Every man needs a spiritual father who guides him in the ways of God, and every man needs to be a spiritual father to someone he influences as well. You should both *have* a spiritual father and *be* a spiritual father. Without this connection, a man can't have the impact God intended him to have on others in the body of Christ.

> *You should both have a spiritual father and be a spiritual father.*

Who in your life needs a spiritual father? When was the last time you had an in-depth conversation with him?

What specifically would you have to change in your life to mentor a younger man?

Kingdom man, get involved in the body of Christ. Get connected. Serve. Lead. Mentor. Pray. Teach. Train. Discover the gifts God has given you and ways those gifts can benefit your church. Are you great at fixing cars? Then consider starting a workshop to train disadvantaged youth so that they can acquire the skills needed to find jobs and get off the streets. Do you have a background in law? Then start or participate in a ministry that moderates disputes according to biblical principles of reconciliation. Do you know computers? Reach out to others in the church or community who can benefit from your expertise. Are you a successful businessman? Then mentor the youth in your church or community by allowing them to spend time with you on the job. The possibilities are endless. And the outcomes are priceless.

As you think about your gifts and abilities, identify at least two ways you can make a difference in the lives of other men or youth.

1.

2.

Beside each action write the name of a young man whose needs it could help meet.

Pray for anyone you have identified as needing the influence of a kingdom man. Pray for an opportunity to engage with him on a deeper level. Then take the initiative of setting up a meeting with him to discuss ways you can provide training and guidance.

Day 4

A Kingdom Man and His Community

The greatest test of the strength of a man, his family, and his church is the health of his community and nation. If kingdom men are at work, a community should steadily improve.

Psalm 128:5 tells us when a man receives His blessings in Zion, Jerusalem will feel the impact:

> *May the Lord bless you from Zion,*
> *so that you will see the prosperity of Jerusalem*
> *all the days of your life.*

When kingdom men are making a difference in their homes and churches, the city and country will also benefit.

What do you consider the top three needs in your community?

1.

2.

3.

Unless we address the man problem in our country, we will not survive. No government program or initiative will succeed in saving our culture and nation if men don't rise up to become kingdom men in their personal lives, in their homes, in their churches, and in their communities. No amount of money will fix the problems we face as a nation. And no amount of legislation will fix what's ultimately a spiritual problem: too many men are out of alignment under the Lord God.

The Old Testament begins with promise and hope: "In the beginning God created ..." (Gen. 1:1). Creation embodies life, breath, and energy. Yet the end of the Old Testament concludes with the taste of disaster: "He will turn the hearts of fathers to their children and the hearts of children to their fathers. Otherwise, I will come and strike the land with a curse" (Mal. 4:6).

Why do you think a nation is cursed unless the hearts of children and fathers are turned toward each other?

Only when men take their rightful place within our culture, becoming the husbands, fathers, and citizens they were created to be, will the atmosphere be radically changed. When a man's heart is turned toward his children, his heart is also turned toward his wife since it is in the best interest of his child that a father loves the child's mother. Likewise, if a man's heart is turned toward his children, his heart is also turned toward the church and community since it is in the best interest of his child that these entities function as God intended.

To have restored communities and a transformed nation, God's people must start to obey His Word and live by kingdom principles. God's men must start being real men instead of simply going through the motions while still living by the standards of the world.

God's men must start being real men instead of simply going through the motions while still living by the standards of the world.

Check the essential ways a kingdom man must live for the King in his culture.

☐ Speak out about the truth of God's Word

☐ Share the gospel

☐ Get involved in politics

☐ Stand up for biblical values

☐ Work to change existing laws

☐ Obey Christ as a father, employee, church member, and citizen

☐ Worship the one true God

There's nothing wrong with political involvement and efforts to legislate justice and morality. Yet kingdom men order their lives according to the values and priorities of the kingdom. When the church starts being divided over political sides, we've missed the kingdom. The kingdom is bigger than politics. It's bigger than government. God's kingdom purposes transcend politics, personal preferences, racial divisions, and all other agendas. Only when citizens of the King operate by the precepts of His kingdom will we see the transformation of the culture.

The culture around us can be transformed only from the inside out. It won't happen through government intervention from the outside in. When the people of Judah were captured and taken into exile in Babylon, God didn't instruct them to overthrow the government or to change the policies of the Babylonians in order to improve their situation. Instead, He told them, "Seek the welfare of the city I have deported you to. Pray to the LORD on its behalf, for when it has prosperity, you will prosper" (Jer. 29:7).

Like the Jews in Babylon, Christians today live in a foreign land. Many of the people, systems, and institutions around us don't promote kingdom values and purposes. Yet God isn't telling us to rebel, to be angry, or to seclude ourselves in our own community of faith. Instead, we are to actively seek the welfare of our towns, states, and nation. Kingdom men can do that when we take an active role in improving our society instead of complaining about it and waiting for someone else to make a difference.

What are you actively doing to seek the prosperity of your community?

Reflect on the three greatest needs of your community you listed earlier today. How can you be involved to bring change to one of those areas?

The lack of kingdom men is the scourge of our day. Their absence has contributed to, if not directly caused, widespread poverty, high dropout rates, imprisonment, drug abuse, teen suicide, and general purposelessness in the rising generation. God's kingdom solution is to introduce positive male influencers into society—men who want to see the kingdom come on earth as it is in heaven.

Pray for your community. Seek its welfare in prayer. Pray about any opportunities you have to make a difference for the kingdom in your community.

Day 5

The Legacy of a Kingdom Man

It sounds daunting, doesn't it, to say a kingdom man's destiny isn't just to live aligned under the lordship of Christ but also to lead his family, to build his church, and eventually to change the world? The truth, though, is that living out that vision is most often accomplished in small ways that eventually add up to something big. One way we, as kingdom men, can most profoundly and positively influence the culture of today and tomorrow is to simply commit ourselves to being fathers to the fatherless.

Read the following verses.

God in His holy dwelling
is a father to the fatherless
and a champion of widows.
Psalm 68:5

Pure and undefiled religion before our God and Father
is this: to look after orphans and widows in their distress
and to keep oneself unstained by the world.
James 1:27

Why do you think God displays an affinity for widows and orphans in Scripture?

Widows and orphans represent people in a society who have no one to protect and provide for them. People in great need hold a special place in God's heart. His nature is to respond to those who readily acknowledge their great need and look to Him as their Father and Provider. If we want to truly live out the values of the kingdom, we must also commit ourselves to the causes God values. We must represent God in our society by being surrogate fathers to people in need.

> *We must represent God in our society by being surrogate fathers to people in need.*

We frequently think of orphans as those who have lost parents, but residing in our society are millions of spiritual orphans, those whose fathers have abandoned them relationally, emotionally, or physically. A child without the positive influence and presence of a father is an orphan. We need to open our eyes to see the multitude of orphans who have been left on their own without anyone to rear them or to speak the truth of God's Word into their lives. Opening our eyes to the existence of the orphans around us will reveal not only a great tragedy but also an incredible opportunity for kingdom men.

In the Book of 1 Chronicles, tucked away in the middle of one genealogy after another, is the model of a mentor who impacted his community as a spiritual father. His name is Asher. Scripture gives us the names of his four sons and one daughter, along with some of their descendants. Then it summarizes, "All these were Asher's sons. They were the heads of their ancestral houses, chosen men, warriors, and chiefs among the leaders" (7:40).

The name *Asher* in Hebrew means *happy* and *blessed*. Because of his influence in the lives of those within his realm, what is recorded about Asher isn't recorded about anyone else in all of the genealogies listed before and after him. Asher's legacy is unique because his sons were "heads of their ancestral houses." Essentially, Asher mentored leaders who were positioned to influence the kingdom as mentors themselves. That's the real end game for a kingdom man.

Describe your legacy as a kingdom man if your life ended today.

153

There's a world of princes in our nation today who have no one to tell them who they can be as kingdom men. No one to lead Bible study with them. No one to take them to church. No one to correct them when they are wrong. No one to teach them how to live life, how to treat a girl, how to be responsible, and how to make wise decisions. The result is spiritual castration. Their royalty has been stripped from them by a culture that doesn't recognize them as princes.

Our nation today needs men who will step up and lead like Asher and his sons, men who will be "heads of their ancestral houses." If that doesn't happen, we will continue to have generations of men who don't know how to take their positions of leadership in the kingdom of God.

Check some options you would consider to mentor young men in your community.

☐ Tutoring teenage boys

☐ Volunteering at youth organizations

☐ Leading a Bible study

☐ Starting a discipleship group

☐ Teaching life skills

☐ Coaching sports teams

☐ Taking young men on a mission trip

☐ Organizing ministry teams

☐ Other:

How would you need to change your schedule to create time for opportunities like these?

Our society's problem isn't solely our government's problem. It's the church's problem. It's our problem as kingdom men. Our mission field isn't merely across the sea. It's across the street in our own Jerusalem and Judea—in Detroit, Dallas, Baltimore, Miami. It's in your local community. We must not look away because it may cost us more than we can afford. It may cost us the futures of our own sons and daughters.

The challenge we face is epic. The battle for morality, values, the family, the economy, health care, education, and the kingdom of God is real. We need bold men of valor to step up and mentor the princes. We need kingdom men who will change the world.

Before our world changes us.

Everyone else is going public. It's time for kingdom men to go public too.

Pray about your responsibility to mentor the next generation of kingdom men. Commit before God to be a spiritual father in one of the ways you have studied today. Pray for courage and initiative to move forward as a kingdom man.

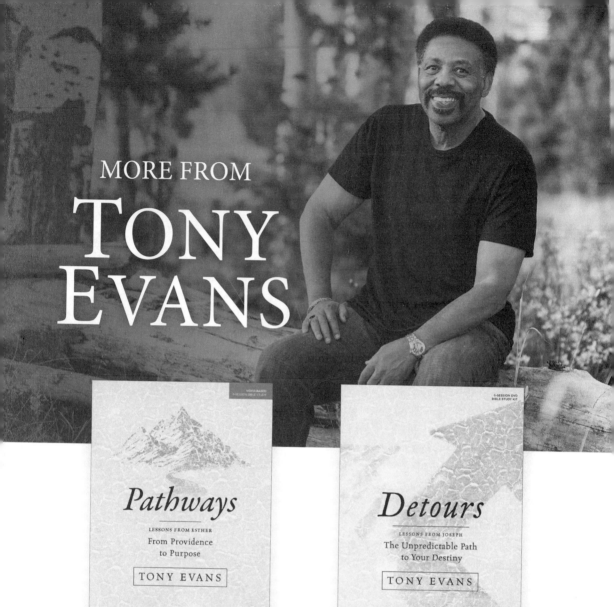

MORE FROM
TONY
EVANS

PATHWAYS
From Providence to Purpose

Use the biblical account of Esther
to discover your own pathway to
purpose as you learn and apply
principles of God's providence.
(6 sessions)

Bible Study Kit $99.99
Bible Study Book $14.99

DETOURS
The Unpredictable Path to Your Destiny

Find hope in understanding that the
sudden or seemingly endless detours
in life are God's way of moving you from
where you are to where He wants you to
be. (6 sessions)

Bible Study Kit $99.99
Bible Study Book $14.99

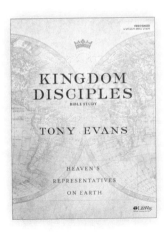

KINGDOM DISCIPLES
Heaven's Representatives on Earth

Develop a confidence and urgency to fulfill your primary responsibility to be a disciple and to make other disciples. (6 sessions)

Bible Study Kit $99.99
Bible Study Book $14.99

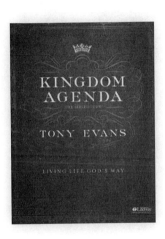

KINGDOM AGENDA
Living Life God's Way

Learn to apply biblical kingdom principles to everyday realities for the individual, the family, the church, or the nation. (6 sessions)

Bible Study Kit $99.99
Bible Study Book $14.99

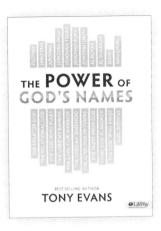

THE POWER OF GOD'S NAMES

Learn the meanings of God's names to know Him more fully and experience Him more deeply. (6 sessions)

Bible Study Kit $99.99
Bible Study Book $14.99

Prices and availability subject to change without notice.

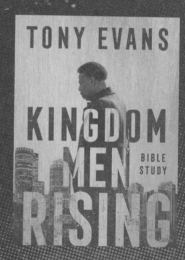

RISE UP

Christian men should be who God has called them to be. This new Bible study will help you assess your current situation and get going on the adventure that God wants you on.

Learn more online or call 800.458.2772.
lifeway.com/kingdommenrising

TONY EVANS

KINGDOM MEN RISING
BIBLE STUDY

Lifeway

TONY EVANS

NO MORE EXCUSES

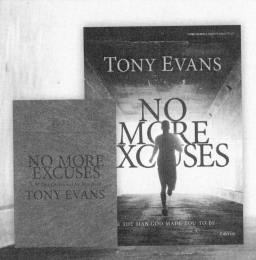

Sometimes circumstances in life make it difficult for men to be all God wants them to be. But Tony Evans urges men to stop looking at their circumstances as excuses and instead to see them as challenges and opportunities for success. Exploring the examples of men of God throughout the Bible, these resources will challenge you to lay down your excuses, stop compromising, and fight to be a man of character and commitment.

ALSO AVAILABLE:
No More Excuses:
A 90-Day Devotional for Men

Lifeway™

Understand your position under God.

Our culture has redefined manhood by emasculating men through a repositioning of the role. Men are portrayed as weak, self-serving, and unfocused. What's a Kingdom man to do?

The Bible clearly communicates that man was created to exercise dominion over the various areas of his life, taking responsibility for himself and others entrusted to his care. When a man functions within the principles of biblical manhood, those around him benefit from his leadership and care. This study challenges and equips men to fully understand their position under God, learning to operate under the authority of Jesus Christ.

- Examine what it means to be a Kingdom man in the world today.

- Understand your roles and responsibilities as a leader in God's kingdom.

- Identify the spheres of influence that God has entrusted to you.

- Get practical ways to advance God's kingdom at home, at church, and in the world.

ADDITIONAL RESOURCES

VIDEO CONTENT
Streamable session videos featuring Tony Evans are included with the purchase price of this book. Look for your access code on the attached insert.

KINGDOM MAN eBOOK
The eBook includes the content of this printed book but offers the convenience and flexibility that comes with mobile technology.

005840638 **$20.99**

More resources can be found online at lifeway.com/kingdomman

Price and availability subject to change without notice.